**W9-BNL-729**

## FILMMAKERS SERIES
*edited by*
Anthony Slide

# SATYAJIT RAY

## In Search of the Modern

Suranjan Ganguly

*Filmmakers Series, no. 73*

**The Scarecrow Press, Inc.**
**Lanham, Maryland • Toronto • Plymouth, UK**
**2007**

SCARECROW PRESS, INC.

Published in the United States of America
by Scarecrow Press, Inc.
A wholly owned subsidary of
The Rowman & Littlefield Publishing Group, Inc.
4501 Forbes Boulevard, Suite 200, Lanham, Maryland 20706
www.scarecrowpress.com

Estover Road
Plymouth PL6 7PY
United Kingdom

British Library Cataloguing in Publication Information Available

The hardback edition of this book was previously cataloged by the
Library of Congress as follows:

Ganguly, Suranjan, 1958–
    Satyajit Ray : in search of the modern / Suranjan Ganguly.
        p. cm. — (Filmmakers series ; no. 73)
    Includes bibliographical references and index.
    Filmography: p.
    ISBN 0-8108-3769-2 (alk. paper)
        1. Ray, Satyajit, 1921–1992—Criticism and interpretation.   I. Title.
    II. Series.

    PN1998.3.R4 G36 2000
    791.43′0233′092—dc21                                        99-056062

ISBN-13: 978-0-8108-5900-5 (pbk. : alk. paper)
ISBN-10: 0-8108-5900-9 (pbk. : alk. paper)

Manufactured in the United States of America

∞™ The paper used in this publication meets the minimum requirements of
American National Standard for Information Sciences—Permanence of
Paper for Printed Library Materials, ANSI/NISO Z39.48–1992.

To Kironmoy Raha

# Contents

# Acknowledgments

My first debt is to the city of Calcutta where most of this book was written during a seven-month stay in 1997 while I was on leave from the University of Colorado at Boulder, where I teach film. The choice of locale was determined not simply by the exigencies of research but also by personal factors. It seemed only fitting that this book should be written in Ray's city—a city to which he was passionately devoted. Moreover, Calcutta is *my* city; I have lived most of my life there and my passion for it is no less than his. Besides—and I couldn't escape this sense of fatedness—the seed of the book was sown there.

For a budding cinephile such as myself, Calcutta in the mid-to-late '70s offered an astonishingly vibrant film culture that was unique to India. There was no dearth of good cinema thanks to the many film clubs, film societies, and foreign consulates that organized weekly screenings of international classics. And there was Ray, whose tall shadow (he was six feet four) extended deep into our lives. The fact that he lived and worked in the city was in itself enormously inspiring to my generation. When he granted me an interview in 1987, it made me think seriously about someday writing a book on him.

Several people in Calcutta were most generous with their help while I was working on this project. I wish to first thank Sandip Ray for assisting me in every possible way with my research and during the actual writing of the book. I could not have undertaken this project without his support. The late Nirmalya Acharya gave me copies of Ray's screenplays published in *Ekshan*, the literary journal that he edited; Lakshman Ghosh of the Ray Archive dug up Bengali film journals for me; Siddhartha Bose provided much-needed assistance with my computer.

I'm very grateful to Kironmoy Raha, Dr. Nita Pillai, and Dr. Indrani Halder for their painstaking reading of the manuscript. This book has benefited immensely from their many helpful suggestions. I would especially like to thank Dr. Pillai for her very instructive critique.

I leaned heavily on the hospitality and support of an extraordinary group of friends—the Lovelock Gang—whom I've known for over twenty years. I would like to express my warmest appreciation to Rakesh and Nandini Batra, Rangeet Raj and Sharoni Mitra, Jasojit and Aparna Mookerjea, and Sanjay and Shuma Raha.

In Boulder, Bruce Kawin's insightful reading of the manuscript made me rethink issues in a substantial way. I'm deeply indebted to him for being so generous with his time and for providing me with some urgent mentoring. I'm very grateful to Jim Palmer for reading an earlier version of two chapters. I would like to thank Stan Brakhage for his friendship and his untiring efforts to keep me cheerful as I struggled with the revisions. His presence has been a vital source of inspiration. I also wish to thank Marian Keane for being such a sincere and caring friend.

I would like to acknowledge the considerable help I have received from the Film Studies staff—Vivienne Palmer, Shirley Carnahan, Pablo Kjolseth, Angella Dirks, and especially Don Yannacito.

I would like to express my gratitude to the University of Colorado for providing me with a Junior Faculty Development Grant that enabled me to do some preliminary research in Calcutta.

The university also awarded me a travel grant to cover my trip to India in 1997 as well as giving me leave from teaching to work on my book.

I would like to thank Anthony Slide and Scarecrow Press for their patience during the final preparation of this manuscript. I would also like to thank Bob Kowkabany for being such a meticulous copyeditor. I wish to acknowledge here that certain portions of this book previously appeared in *Film Criticism*, *The Journal of South Asian Literature*, and *The Journal of Commonwealth Literature*.

My sincere thanks to two Ray scholars, Darius Cooper and Cuthbert Lethbridge, who shared with me their ideas, resources, and, above all, their enthusiasm for Ray. I would also like to thank the students who enrolled in my Asian cinema courses—especially my course on Ray and Kurosawa—for their valuable input.

I would like to take this opportunity to express my gratitude to the following who, in more ways than they know, helped to make this book happen: Sunanda Basu, Forrest Williams, Lucile Zellar, Miranda Thompson, Pradip Bhaumik, and Jai Vora.

Last but not least, my thanks to my mother for being so extraordinary in every way, and to Sangeeta whom I met during the writing of this book and whose enthusiasm and support provided me with that extra boost to reach the finishing line.

# Introduction

**A** s the man credited with ushering modernity into the tradition-bound Indian cinema, Satyajit Ray remains an enigmatic figure. Classicist? Humanist? The last Bengali Renaissance man? None of these labels fits him well. His films, likewise, defy easy formulations. While almost all of them are rooted within Ray's Bengali milieu and made primarily for Bengalis, they are transcultural in their larger implications. Moreover, they display such diverse influences as Italian neorealism, Renoir, Mozart, Bonnard, and Cartier-Bresson. While they have been shaped by Ray's cosmopolitan, modernist, twentieth-century perspective, they reveal a value system that has more to do with the nineteenth century. Such paradoxes are common in a cinema generated within a postcolonial society, especially one that is characterized by bewildering diversity. Ray's upbringing and cultural

1

inheritance make the situation all the more complex since he is the product of a unique East–West fusion. As the sociologist Ashis Nandy has remarked, "Ray . . . lived with a plurality of selves, and a part of him was as deeply Indian as a part of him was Western."[1] Thus, his struggle to define himself within the framework of his legacy involves a larger struggle to define the India within which he functions as an artist.

Ray was born in Calcutta in 1921 into a middle-class family of writers, painters, and poets. The family had strong links to the Bengali Renaissance, a nineteenth-century cultural movement based on a synthesis of Western liberal ideas and traditional Eastern values. (The chapter on *Charulata* provides a detailed discussion of the Renaissance.) The high priests of the Renaissance promoted education, science and rationality, widow remarriage, emancipation of women, and the reform of religion. Ray thus inherited the worldview of a class deeply committed to the European Enlightenment philosophies of progress, which would shape the liberal-humanist idealism of his work. The city, where the Renaissance was forged, would also be a factor in his evolution. Although no longer the capital of British India at the time of his birth, Calcutta was still the country's most cosmopolitan city as well as its foremost cultural center, with a vibrant intellectual life. Within its urban colonial milieu Ray would encounter a modernity that was a direct result of the East–West fusion.

As a child, Ray had already displayed a prodigious gift for drawing. His education in a school where the medium of instruction was English exposed him to Western literature as well as science. In his mid-teens he developed a passion for Western classical music, especially for Beethoven. Around the same time, he became a cinephile and rarely missed the Hollywood films by Lubitsch, Capra, Wyler, Stevens, Ford, Wilder, and others that were shown in the city. In 1940 Ray shifted to Shantiniketan, about 100 miles from Calcutta, and enrolled as a student of fine arts at the university set up by the poet and Nobel laureate, Rabindranath Tagore. It was the turning point in his life. As he put it, "I was not conscious of any roots in Bengal at all. That happened in Shantiniketan."[2] Tagore, who was the most prominent figure of the Bengali Renaissance and a close family friend, had conceived of his university as a meeting place for the world. There could be no better symbol of an East–West blend. Its motto in English meant "Where the world makes its home in a nest." As Ray studied under teachers such as Nandalal Bose and Benode Behari Mukherjee, who advocated an intrinsically Indian approach to art, he became aware of the inadequacies of his colonial education. As he later recalled, "the place had opened windows for me. More than anything else, it had brought to me an awareness of our tradition, that I knew would serve as a foundation for any branch of art that I wished to pursue."[3]

But the West would continue to play a conspicuous role in all his major deliberations, even after India achieved independence in 1947. Back in Calcutta, Ray began his career in a British advertising firm and became its art director within a very short time. In 1949 he met Jean Renoir, who was in India to shoot *The River* (1951)—a meeting that inspired him to think seriously of making a film someday. Then, in 1950 in London, he saw Vittorio De Sica's *Bicycle Thief* (1949), and his mind was made up. Italian neorealism had offered him a model for a film that would be set in the heart of rural Bengal. On his way back to India, he began to draft the screenplay of *Pather Panchali/Song of the Little Road* (1955), which would revolutionize Indian film and place it on the map of international cinema.

The cosmopolitanism that becomes evident in this short overview of Ray's formative years underlies all his films. However, it becomes most apparent in his attempt to define the modern as a specific hybrid discourse. As a postcolonial, Ray cannot avoid the compulsion to examine the contexts that have shaped his identity as an artist inhabiting multiple worlds. As he claimed, "I want to show, not just single aspects of our life today, like contemporary politics, but a broader view of Indian history."[4] This search manifests itself in his persistent efforts to describe the making of a nation as it emerges from its feudal past and its experience with colonialism to become a new hybrid, postcolonial entity. For Ray, the modern is inseparable from this sense of the plural that incorporates within itself its history of multiple dislocations. Thus what seems at first an East–West cosmopolitanism turns out to be a complex, all-encompassing discourse in which Ray seeks to find a pattern within diversity. As Amartya Sen explains, "While Satyajit Ray insists on retaining the real cultural features of the society that he portrays, his view of India . . . is full of recognition of a complex reality with immense heterogeneity at every level."[5]

Ray's career as a filmmaker began during the heady years of nation-building under India's first prime minister, Jawaharlal Nehru. The India Nehru envisaged was a progressive, secular, industrialized democracy. Its modernity lay in its dynamic fusion of past and present and its ability to assimilate highly divergent traditions and ideologies while remaining a single, unified nation. Nehru, who had studied at Harrow and Cambridge but whose mentors were Gandhi and Tagore, subscribed to the same liberal-humanist, cosmopolitan agenda as Ray. His India, as Judith Brown writes, was conceived as "a composite nation that included a great diversity of peoples and reflected a many-layered sense of 'being Indian' that grew out of the subcontinent's long history of dealing with outsiders. . . ."[6] Despite the partition of the country in 1947, he retained his vision of a national identity "born of diversity and sustained by tolerance and secularism."[7]

Such a vision of inclusiveness coincided with Ray's notion of culture as a hybrid in which diverse historical and social components retain their separateness while forming an integrated whole. Nehru proved to be a mentor whom Ray would admire for his "liberalism . . . a certain awareness of Western values and a fusion of Eastern and Western values."[8] It was left to artists like him to translate Nehru's dream into reality through art. To do so was also to legitimize a specific sociohistorical space within which the artist was able to engage in his or her art-making. Thus Ray set out to portray the modern

Indian experience—integral both to his identity as Indian as well as to his status as artist. His films would address the citizens of a newly independent nation who sought to comprehend, like him, what it meant to be modern.

The films from *Pather Panchali* onwards become an extended study of an emerging nation as filtered through the experiences of men and women who seek to define themselves in relation to the larger forces that are transforming their world. Usually, these forces manifest themselves through fairly basic conflicts between the feudal and the modern, tradition and progress, the village and the city, the old and the new. Even if Ray offers no easy resolutions, we sense how these conflicts are shaping a modern composite identity that for him represents true Indianness. Thus while he focuses on a host of different issues and problems in his films, it is always in relation to an India that is in a perpetual state of growth as a dynamic, pluralistic nation.

This would become more apparent if one were to ignore the chronology of Ray's oeuvre and rearrange the films. Ray's history of India would then begin with *Shatranj ki Khilari/The Chess Players* (1977), in which feudalism is pitted against colonialism as the British seek to annex the northern Indian province of Oudh in 1856. In *Charulata* (1964), set a few years later in 1879, India is now officially part of the British Empire. The new reciprocity between East and West is evident in the Bengali Renaissance that forms the backdrop to the story of a woman's awakening within a patriarchal society. Both these studies of the nineteenth century are supplemented by *Devi/The Goddess* (1960) in which the Hindu religious orthodoxy of the 1860s finds a vocal critic in a Western-educated man who subscribes to the new philosophy of progressive rationalism. *Ghare Baire/The Home and the World* (1984), although set in 1905, marks the close of the nineteenth century as the Swadeshi Movement is launched against British imperialism (ironically enough, the British were responsible for implanting the idea of nationalism through Western education). Thus, significantly, Ray goes no further back than the nineteenth century and associates the birth of modernity with the coming of the white man and his impact on a traditional society. Virtually all his subsequent films would allude directly or indirectly to these facts.

The Apu trilogy (1955–59), for example, comes to mind at once, since it places Apu's growth within an India being changed by education, the railroad, and migrations from the village to the city. *Jalsaghar/The Music Room* (1958), a study of the decay of feudalism, focuses on a landed aristocrat in British India who is about to be upstaged by the new mercantile class. The films set in post–Independence India such as *Kanchanjungha* (1962), *Aranyer Din Ratri/Days and Nights in the Forest* (1970), and the Calcutta trilogy (1970–75) all deal with the effects of neocolonialism in a country where power is wielded by a Western-educated elite.

One could point to other examples as well, but it is necessary here to make a distinction between the films Ray produced during Nehru's lifetime and those produced after Nehru's death in 1964. It can certainly be argued that the films made between 1955 and 1964 strongly endorse Nehru's nation-building. There is an idealism that borders on the romantic as Ray upholds values such as education (*Aparajito/The Unvanquished*, 1956), the family as a social unit (*Pather Panchali*), and the emancipation of women (*Charulata* and *Mahanagar /The Big City*, 1963) and critiques feudalism (*Jalsaghar*) and orthodoxy (*Devi*), which stand in the way of a progressive modernity. It is in this phase that we encounter a body of work that has been described as "an enlightened liberal's perception of the history of modern India."[9] By setting his films mostly in the past, Ray provides a historical basis for his overall optimism. The modern is not conceived in terms of a violent rupture with the past; instead, it emerges through a dynamic relationship with the past. Ray not only traces the lineage of the modern but points to its future as he connects past and present. Thus the films assert that Nehru's vision of economic growth and social reconstruction is historically valid.

Like other artists of his generation, Ray found it increasingly difficult to sustain such idealism as India rapidly succumbed to corruption and bureaucratic inefficiency in the post–Nehruvian era. There was now no going back to the past to trace the constituents of the dream; it was time to come to terms with its brutal aftermath. Henceforth, most of Ray's films would address problems within the contemporary world as if to compensate for some of his earlier naive optimism. Beginning with *Aranyer Din Ratri* through *Jana Aranya/ The Middle Man* (1975), the last film in the Calcutta trilogy, Ray would repeatedly focus on the urban scene and the emasculation of the Indian male along with the reformulation of women's roles in post–Independence India.

These are the most cynical of his films, tracing the moral and spiritual decline of a society from which all hope seems to have been expunged. As in his earlier work, here too he would investigate the ethical consequences of change, singling out instances of compromise and betrayal. Even in his last three films, that are all set in the present— *Ganashatru/An Enemy of the People* (1989), *Shakha Proshakha/Branches of a Tree* (1990), and *Agantuk/The Stranger* (1991)—he would continue to focus on an India that had altered almost beyond recognition. Despite an overlay of hope, these films, which constitute his final testament, display a profound disillusionment. As Ashis Rajadhyaksha observes: "[T]his India—inducted into a global market on terms set by US trade representatives—was not entering the place in the world he had sought in the heraldic '50s when he made *Pather Panchali*." [10]

This book focuses on Ray's negotiations with the modern in six of his major films made between 1955 and 1970—*Pather Panchali, Aparajito, Apur Sansar/The World of Apu* (1959), *Charulata, Aranyer Din Ratri,* and *Pratidwandi/The Adversary* (1970). The first four were made during the Nehru years, while *Aranyer Din Ratri* and *Pratidwandi* belong to the politically turbulent '70s. The films are pivotal in that they not only describe some of the major shifts within Ray's thinking about the modern, but define certain key issues within his discourse of modernity. This is not to suggest that these are the *only* films or the *only* issues that are relevant. Films such as *Jalsaghar, Devi, Kanchanjungha*, and *Mahanagar* could certainly find a place in such a study as this. But this book does not seek to provide an overview of Ray's cinema from the mid-'50s to the '70s; rather, it examines in detail some of the more significant moments in his oeuvre to suggest the nature of an ongoing, lifelong project. It should here be pointed out that this book is written primarily for a Western audience familiar with Ray's films but unable to engage with their sociohistorical contexts. This explains the limited attention given to the aesthetics of Ray's cinema. A future project will address the poetics of Ray's films at length.

All six films refer to Ray's abiding interest in how a culture acquires a composite, hybrid shape through its encounter with history and modernity. While this approach provides the book with a larger framework within which it can function, its primary goal is to identify those experiences that Ray defines as modern. Thus the first and second chapters, which deal with the Apu trilogy, focus on his preoccupation with subjectivity in contexts such as education, urban culture, and the management of grief. The section on *Charulata*, that describes a woman's burgeoning sense of self within a male world, foregrounds the female gaze as well as writing as a form of female discourse. The chapter on *Aranyer Din Ratri* focuses on the post-colonial mind as four men, out on a holiday from the city, reinvent India in English. Finally, the book offers a reading of *Pratidwandi* as a film in which Ray contemplates the nature of action in a society suspended between apathy and revolution.

While such issues form the core of each chapter, it is not to the exclusion of other related concerns. This book makes a special effort to address Ray's modernist preoccupation with language and reflexivity—two issues that have received scant attention from critics. Despite his commitment to a cinema close to reality, Ray displays in his major work a complex awareness of film as artifice. However, he abstains from the aggressive self-referentiality of a filmmaker such as Godard, or, closer to home, Mrinal Sen. There are no authorial intrusions or narrative discontinuities in Ray's work, no display of cinematic apparatus or foregrounding of technique for the sake of technique; neither does he seek to subvert his viewers' expectations or disrupt their viewing experience. Instead, as in the Apu trilogy and *Charulata*, through allusions to the literary and performing arts, to the act of reading and writing in particular, and to issues such as spectatorship and the politics of the gaze, he makes us aware of the formation of a construct and our collective participation in it. Perhaps there is in such reflexivity an attempt to proclaim film as an art form as distinct from film as a commercial product. In Ray's early work such a distinction reveals his self-consciousness as an artist seeking to remake cinema in Nehru's new India. There is a sense that only through the forging of a new cinematic idiom can the story of India's modernity be truly narrated.

Ray's emphasis of language serves to reinforce the notion of artifice, but he also explores language in its larger social and political connotations. In *Aranyer Din Ratri* he shows how in a postcolonial society the language of the ex-colonizer is appropriated by the elite so that they can rewrite India to fit their agenda. He also describes the formation of a hybrid culture through the creation of a new language in which Bengali is mixed freely with English. But more often, Ray focuses on the deceptions people practice through words as they invest in the illusory rather than facing reality. Both *Apur Sansar* and *Charulata* make multiple references to books and writing to suggest how characters tend to confuse the line separating art from life.

Overall, this book seeks to convey Ray's belief that the modern is best understood as a total experience in relation to how people feel, think, and act—in short, how they express themselves within a changing society. But the task is not made any easier by the fact that India is a society of extreme contrasts and paradoxes that has existed for nearly 5,000 years. Some of the questions that Ray's films pose are: Is it always possible to distinguish the modern from the traditional or are they just two sides of the same coin? Does the modern simply embody the contradictory nature of contemporary Indian experience? Or is the modern all about becoming the modern—always in the making—at best, a form of acute self-consciousness?

The problem is further compounded by the fact that Ray's value system is of nineteenth-century origin. He has repeatedly used words such as "universal" and "timeless" to describe his work and alluded to the philosophy of the Upanishads to explain his concern with diversity and pattern. Such terms of reference can be traced to the Bengali Renaissance, to Tagore, and even further back. Given this respect for traditional values, how modern, then, is Ray's modernity? And against what is this modernity to be measured? This book seeks to grapple with some of these issues.

## Notes

1. Ashis Nandy, "How 'Indian' is Ray?" *Cinemaya* 20 (1993): 43.

2. Satyajit Ray, "My Life, My Work," in *Satyajit Ray: A Portrait in Black and White*, ed. Tarapada Banerjee (New Delhi: Viking, 1993), 17.

3. Ibid., 19.

4. Karuna Shankar Roy, "The Artist in Politics: An Interview with Satyajit Ray." *Drama Review* 15, no. 2 (1971): 310.

5. Amartya Sen, "Our Culture, Their Culture." *Telegraph* (Calcutta) (January 1, 1996): 8.

6. Judith Brown, "The Jewel without the Crown." *Bloomsbury Review* (February 15, 1998): 28.

7. Ibid., 28.

8. Folke Issakson, "Conversation with Satyajit Ray." *Sight and Sound* 39, no. 3 (1970): 120.

9. Samik Bandyopadhyay, "Introduction," in *Satyajit Ray: A Film by Shyam Benegal*, ed. Alakananda Datta and Samik Bandyopadhyay (Calcutta: Seagull Books, 1988), v.

10. Ashis Rajadhyaksha, "Beyond Orientalism." *Sight and Sound* 2, no. 4 (1992): 35.

*one*

# The Apu Trilogy:
# Slate and Globe

The Apu trilogy, it could be argued, is the first work of the Indian cinema that shifts the emphasis from exteriority to interiority. Not that other films had not invested in psychological realism before—especially in the Bengali cinema—but in most cases such renderings were either highly literary or compromised by commercial demands. By foregrounding consciousness and subjectivity through a complex visual language of symbol, nuance, and gesture, Ray introduced a new discourse within Indian cinema. The modernity of the trilogy lies precisely in this: That Ray tells Apu's story not within a melodramatic framework but in terms of an evolving male consciousness that seeks to define itself in relation to a changing world. And he makes India the setting for this cinematic *Bildungsroman*, thereby combining two narratives: One, of an emerging modern sensibility, and the other of a country emerging from its feudal and colonial past into the twentieth century. As Chidananda Das Gupta writes, we experience through Apu "the inevitable movement of one era into another."[1] Thus his growth from childhood to manhood encapsulates the conflicts, paradoxes, and histories of a nation in the making.

As the prototype of the sensitive, rational, and self-conscious man whose identity is shaped by a series of real and symbolic dislocations, Apu is very much a product of his time. He undergoes no less than four major physical displacements in the trilogy, of which the most far-reaching in consequence is his move to the city. In an India being rapidly transformed by technology and Western education, such disruptions affirm the dynamic nature of growth. Apu's journeys come to exemplify the complex interface between tradition and modernity, freedom and responsibility, individualism and community. We see this in the way his search for independence involves a radical reformulation of his duties and obligations toward his family. The shift to Calcutta is also a shift away from his father's profession as priest as well as from his widowed mother, who is left to die alone. Throughout the trilogy there is a dialectic between the alienating solitude of the city and a life lived in close proximity to nature, home, family, and community. Progress, Apu discovers, comes with a price.

Ray makes education the center of Apu's growth, both as a mode of academic study and an empirical experience. In *Aparajito/ The Unvanquished* (1956), Apu's sense of the world expands significantly as he pursues, among other subjects, English and the sciences. Once he relocates to the city, he begins to identify increasingly with its plural, hybrid colonial culture. Such concrete developments throughout the trilogy are complemented by Apu's more intangible and often epiphanic discoveries associated with wonder. There are numerous shots of him observing, thinking, reacting—a whole internal process that Ray traces without ignoring its social and cultural ramifications.

We become aware of a consciousness not only grappling with a wide range of experiences, but learning to make significant choices based on what it assimilates. Ray singles out such self-defining moments when Apu formulates a particular stance in relation to an event or makes a crucial decision within contexts that involve family, education, marriage, displacement, and above all, death.

There are as many as five deaths in the trilogy and they all affect Apu in some manner. The second half of *Apur Sansar/The World of Apu* (1959), in fact, is a prolonged meditation on the management of grief caused by the sudden demise of Apu's wife. For Ray, suffering becomes an index to growth; Apu, who faces the economic uncertainties of a life lived in extreme poverty, must also come to terms with the tragic nature of existence itself. His "education" will be complete only when he can transform his experience of loss into something meaningful. Thus Ray not only emphasizes Apu's rational outlook determined by school and college, but also his emotional life since, for him, the two must necessarily complement each other. How Apu measures up positively, with mind and heart, to the challenge of living, how he moves forward toward self-knowledge and self-liberation become the ultimate test of his modernity.

While this chapter will define the relationship between Apu's subjectivity and his formal education, the next chapter will focus on his "other" education, shaped by the absence of his father, solitude in the city, marriage, and his profound experience of death and suffering. Both chapters seek to describe some of the key stages in the growth of his consciousness from its epiphanic birth to its state of mature self-reflection at the end of *Apur Sansar*. What this study hopes to identify is a burgeoning modernity that even as it presses forward is aligned to the past. Apu's ambivalent attitude toward change—endorsing it while retaining his hold on time-honored values—is shared by many of Ray's protagonists, who also struggle to "emerge from the depths of two millennia of tradition."[2] Ray is clearly more interested in the ambiguities of such a situation than in describing the predictable conflicts within a society in transition.

Apu's deliberations only confirm the problem of defining the modern in terms of binaries; instead, Ray seeks to bring to the fore its composite nature, which incorporates issues and experiences that are often mutually incompatible. The formation of Apu's subjectivity needs to be placed within such a framework.

Ray's trilogy, based on the novels *Pather Panchali* and *Aparajito* by Bibhuti Bhushan Banerjee, begins with Apu's birth in *Pather Panchali/ Song of the Little Road* (1955). The film, set in the early years of the century, takes place in the village of Nischindipur. The Brahmin family consists of father: Harihar, priest and playwright; mother: Sarbojaya; elder sister: Durga; and grand-aunt: Indir. Desperately poor, the family survives on Harihar's frugal income. Apu's growth as a boy is described in terms of such formative experiences as learning to read, glimpsing his first train, witnessing the death of Indir, and finally being uprooted from home and hearth. When Harihar goes off seeking work, the family comes close to starvation. It is during his absence that Durga catches cold in the rain and dies. The film ends with the family's leaving their village for good.

The second film, *Aparajito*, opens in Benaras, where the family's fortunes have improved. But Harihar dies shortly after the film begins, and Sarbojaya finds work as a cook. Apu, now about ten, does odd jobs for the same family. Sensing that her son has no future, Sarbojaya decides to shift with Apu to the village of Mansapota where her uncle lives. Apu begins his training as a priest, but his ambition is to go to school. With the money Sarbojaya has saved, Apu not only enrolls in the local school but excels in his studies. In fact, he is awarded a scholarship to study in Calcutta. Now seventeen, he sets out for the city, leaving Sarbojaya behind. The last half of the film focuses on the gradual estrangement between mother and son that culminates in her death alone, pining for Apu.

In *Apur Sansar*, Apu, now in his early twenties, lives by himself in Calcutta and dreams of literary success. When his friend, Pulu, invites him to his cousin Aparna's wedding at their ancestral country house, Apu goes along. But the bridegroom turns out to be mad, and Apu rescues Aparna from ostracism by marrying her. They have a happy marriage, but when she dies during childbirth he is distraught with grief. For five years he wanders from place to place, mourning Aparna's death. Finally, at Pulu's instigation, he visits his son whom he has never seen before. The film closes with Apu reunited with his son, back on the road where we saw him at the end of the two earlier films.

## Apu's Book

There is a scene early in *Apur Sansar* in which Apu describes to Pulu the novel he's writing. It's a key moment, since the book encapsulates much of the story of the trilogy. Moreover, Apu is displaying his intense self-consciousness by writing his own life into fiction. The parallels are so obvious that Pulu exclaims, "A novel? Why, this is an autobiography!"

Apu's protagonist is a priest's son who decides not to adopt his father's profession when he dies but quits village for city to obtain an education. A man of intellect and ambition, he turns to his rational and scientific faculties in order to overcome "old superstitions" and "orthodoxy." Since he will not accept anything "blindly," he submits everything to reason. However, his search for knowledge is balanced by sensitivity and imagination. Like Apu, he can respond to the world around him with wonder: "Little things move him, give him joy." But he remains poor in the city. Success eludes him and "he does nothing great." And yet, for Apu what counts is that he "never turns away from life" and admits defeat. Instead, he believes that happiness lies in the act of living itself. Apu almost shouts with emotion—"He wants to *live!*"

What stands out in this scene is Apu's ability to define himself in relation to time and project into the future. Perhaps even more significant is his attempt to author his life according to a blueprint that he invents. While he describes his own past with a certain measure of fidelity, it remains to be seen whether life will bear out his idealism about the future. Can he live up to his smug prediction that there is no running away, no "escape" from the vicissitudes of living? Will life imitate art? We notice how careful he is to single out only those aspects that cater to his romantic self-definition. What he leaves out becomes equally crucial in this revealing self-portrait.

Apu's book is the most prominent of many references to the literary and performing arts in the trilogy. Starting with *Pather Panchali*, we notice Ray's attempt to emphasize the artifice of his work. The film's relationship to the *panchali*—folk song or ballad—is implicit in the title itself. The handwritten credits appear on parchment that confirms the literary metaphor and also emphasizes Ray's authorship. Both oral and written forms thus are invoked, and Ray will add to them Indir's song, the schoolteacher's dictation, Durga's incantation as she prays, the priest's recital from the scriptures, and the *jatra* or folk play that Apu watches. By placing his own film in relation to these timeless, indigenous forms, Ray juxtaposes a twentieth-century Western invention—the cinema—and thereby seeks to extend India's artistic heritage. The film we watch proves how a Western import can document an Indian reality and capture its "Indianness." Ray also demonstrates what film is by comparing it to the literary and theatrical while, at the same time, affirming its composite nature that incorporates all these elements. *Aparajito* and *Apur Sansar* are likewise full of allusions, although they are mostly literary and placed within the context of Apu's education and love of literature.

By choosing to include his most important reflexive device—Apu's book—in the final film, Ray insists on the fictionality of the entire trilogy. It becomes his summing up of the trilogy's story as told to us so far. Despite his commitment to realism, he categorically informs us that the trilogy as a cinematic work is a construct, an authored text, and that he has "written" his "book." (It needs to be pointed out here that in Bengali the popular word for film is *boi* [book].) Thus in this last film, he inscribes his own signature over it and proclaims his authorship of the total work. While he never subverts the realism he so carefully builds up, he makes us reflect on its nature and limitations. In the end, the man who modeled his trilogy on Italian neorealism acknowledges that realism is only a skin stretched tightly over elaborate artifice.

## Apu Opens His Eye

The birth of Apu's consciousness takes place shortly after the film begins and is distinguished from his "real" birth. Earlier shots had shown him as a newborn with his mother, and later being rocked by Indir. In the scene where we first see him, he lies within a makeshift hut—the labor room—next to his mother, watched over by women both on and off screen. When Indir comes to visit her grandnephew, one of the women asks her to *see* Apu. We cut to Indir in medium shot, and our first glimpse of him is from her perspective. In other words, Ray avoids the third-person objectifying look and offers a more intimate subjective shot that significantly is seen through a woman's eyes. Indir responds with "lovely boy" and wipes away her tears of joy. Her point of view comes to represent a larger female point of view as a whole community looks on with pride at the child they have helped to bring into the world. Through a process of looking, displaying the baby, and shedding of tears, the women acknowledge the renewal of community and Apu's status as a male child.

In a film that will repeatedly use point-of-view shots and shots of eyes engaged in looking, the invitation to Indir to see Apu is also extended to us so that we may acknowledge his birth. The display of his face symbolizes not only his human presence but his latent consciousness as well. It is a face which, at this point, is without shape or contour. Apu sleeps, his eyes closed, seen by the world but unable to see. Curled up next to his mother, he exists within time and yet out of time. This birth, which establishes a biological fact—his existence—still needs a more profound one that will establish his essence.

In the shot where Apu is being rocked by Indir on the porch, the deep-focus composition links him to the rest of the family grouped together in the kitchen. This is the first time that we see them as a unit, although space divides Indir and Apu from the others. The conversation between Harihar and Sarbojaya practically constitutes an oral history of their deprivation and want. It opens with an allusion to food, then shifts to work, labor, and money—the very fundamentals that govern their existence. Against this recital of family woes that Apu is doomed to inherit, the boy sleeps apart, his eyes still closed, rocked by an ancient woman singing a lullaby. Still ensconced within the maternal and timeless, he is spared the knowledge of his place within the world being described. Thus deprived of the pleasure and pain of consciousness, Apu looks terribly vulnerable, but it is balanced by *our* sense of family, community, and history, all of which seek to draw him in.

When Apu opens his eye, it is a supremely epiphanic moment celebrated with a burst of music. In a two-shot, Durga steals upon him sleeping and stretches a tear in the sheet covering his face to reveal his closed eye. She pries it open with her fingers and pushes aside the sheet. From the close-up of the eye, Ray cuts to a one-shot of Apu sitting up in bed, revealing himself to us. Six years have gone by (the sequence opens with a reference to time as Sarbojaya asks Durga to wake him up so he won't be late for school) and we see a fully formed face and two powerfully alive eyes.

Thus the one-shot isolates and frames Apu in a way that proclaims his independence and self-consciousness while affirming his connectedness to the community his mother and sister (women again) offer him. Unlike the scene where we first viewed him as a baby, this time the third-person camera looks at him. The world gazes at him and he, in turn, looks at the world (and us). The shot defines him as an active and conscious agent whose sense of self—"I"—will be inseparable from his sense of being an "eye." For Ray, this unfolding of consciousness heralds Apu's second and more significant birth. Although we will not witness the trilogy exclusively through Apu's eyes, how he reacts to what he sees will shape our awareness of his world.[3] Also, since our participation is solicited right from the start we never lose our sense of being a collective eye "seeing more than he does, spying on him as it were."[4] At the same time, while Ray defines the independence of Apu's eye, we are not allowed to forget that his space is communal. In the next few shots we see his notion of community assume a concrete form as his mother tucks in the folds of his dhoti at his waist, Durga combs his hair, wipes his mouth after he drinks from a bowl of milk, and then escorts him to school. Ray beautifully evokes the growth of an evolving sense of self and its enclosure within a community, without which it cannot function.

## Apu's Education

Given Ray's cultural inheritance, it makes perfect sense that he should assign a special function to education and associate it with progress and emancipation. If ancient India regarded education as essential to man's moral and spiritual upliftment, Ray's Bengali Renaissance mentors upheld learning as a means of reforming orthodox Hindu society. In their quest for modernity they favored a Western liberal education that could forge a truly progressive outlook. Ray not only fully endorses this ideal but even defines the urge to study, which Apu exhibits, as distinctly modern. Apu's move to the city becomes proof of a vibrant consciousness that finds the rural milieu inhibiting and seeks to further itself. Through his need to "learn, to widen his experience and reach out to a richer existence in which his potentialities can develop more fully,"[5] he displays a self-awareness that for Ray is new and dynamic. Ray doesn't simply focus on this consciousness-forming process that shapes Apu's choices; he also shows how it affects those who are close to him. Thus we not only get a sense of the modern impulse toward education but also the upheavals it causes within a traditional set-up.

Apu's first experience of education is in *Pather Panchali* in the village school run by the local grocer who combines business with teaching. Finding Apu grinning, he admonishes the boy. Does he think this is a playhouse? Apu's answer would probably be in the affirmative given the raised dais on which the grocer-teacher "performs" and the resulting comedy that accompanies his histrionics.

The medium close-ups of Apu's face show him watching, absorbing, but clearly not relishing his first contact with this playhouse-academia where students learn by rote. When a boy is hauled up for playing knots and crosses and is brutally caned, Ray cuts to a reaction shot of a petrified Apu watching the beating—perhaps his first dislocating experience of the adult world. We never see him at the school again, although we know he continues to attend. Clearly a boy of his sensitivity needs less than the schoolhouse can offer, with its emphasis on dogma and discipline.

The next time we see him, slate in hand, the spatial setting has changed dramatically. He sits on his porch at home with his family around him, his feeling of community restored, taking lessons from his father. There is a strong sense here of knowledge handed down from one generation to another as well as an awareness of Apu's privileged position as Brahmin that entitles him to an education. Ray is careful to define the more traditional chores of the other relatives, who are significantly all women: Indir threads a needle while Sarbojaya combs Durga's hair. Only the two males are engaged in writing. Harihar glances occasionally at Apu's slate and gives him words to write while he works on a play. Apu thus learns to write in an atmosphere that is intimate and congenial relative to that of the school.

The sequence is mostly in long take, highlighting the solidarity of the family while hinting at Apu's sense of being simultaneously within and without this familial space. He cannot but be subconsciously aware of his special status, his difference as a male from the women who take care of him but who are debarred from the privileges of the slate. Thus the slate subtly empowers him with its connotations of caste and power. It is also his first writing material; it will later be replaced by the pages of his novel. Thus the scene points to a future that will be shaped by it.

Apu's sense of the world outside is signaled by the sound of the train and the camera tracking close to his face to register his look of wonder. It prompts him to ask Durga whether she has ever glimpsed this mysterious object and whether they can go and see it some day.

As he turns to her, we are very conscious of his hand with the chalk poised over the slate. One day such epiphanies will find a place in the thinly disguised fictional account of his life. For the moment, the train introduces a new perspective, "evoking a world of knowledge and achievement"[6] that the children cannot rationalize but that is enforced by the immediate context of education. The sequence ends with the camera tracking away from the family, its sense of "precise symmetry"[7] still intact, but we know that Apu has sensed another space that will enfold him someday. The scene anticipates the moment when he will catch the train to the city, when the solidarity on the porch will become a distant memory.

In the first half of *Aparajito*, Apu, living in Benaras, does not go to school. In fact, Sarbojaya complains that he has become a monkey—never at home, running wild with the neighborhood boys. But as we see him exploring the embankments of the city, we sense a strong interactive consciousness at work. Apu has not lost any of his capacity for wonder. We also find out that he is learning English from his friend, Sambhu. When his father asks him to translate a Bengali phrase, he comes up with the correct English rendition: "Apu is a good boy." We sense Harihar's pride as the priest's son from the village defines his self-worth in a foreign language. The moment, like the one on the porch, points to the future—English will provide Apu with the key to unlock the world. It also acquires a certain historicity, since this is the first time that he displays his familiarity with the colonizer's language. It broaches the question of identity: Will the adult Apu in future judge himself "a good boy" in English, as determined by English standards? We are made to recall Nehru's vision of cosmopolitanism that begins at home with one's national identity firmly in place prior to any engagement with the West. As we shall see, Apu will live up to this ideal as being first a Bengali before anything else, his self-worth always determined by his immediate cultural context.

After mother and son shift from Benares to Mansapota, we see Apu being trained to be a priest—his new education. While he performs the appropriate rituals, the boys in the village attend school. In one of his most eloquent nonverbal sequences, Ray gives us a sense of Apu's bottled-up energy and how it would atrophy if he were to spend the rest of his life as a priest.

He opens the sequence with Apu walking home after performing his duties while noisily the boys play on the other side of a field. Their infectious high spirits contrast with his more restrained gait. Apu smiles and keeps glancing at them. After he enters his house and exits the frame, the camera stays fixed on the open door; Apu reenters the frame still dressed as a priest, then runs through the door into the space outside. Within the continuum of the long take, Ray enforces the dichotomy between open and closed spaces—a leitmotif that runs throughout the film.

As Apu breaks into a run toward the boys, Ray cuts to a low-angle shot of his going down an embankment and then over a bridge. We again sense two disparate spatial settings and Apu's instinctive preference for openness and freedom. The tracking camera describes all the energy he can unleash in a single bound, an energy that militates against the inert sitting posture in which we've seen him perform as priest. There is a fine sense of different worlds and identities colliding, the timeless India of religion and ritual versus the small universe of the district school where the sciences are taught along with English. As Apu, dressed in his priest's outfit, follows the boys and watches them run toward the school building, he embodies the struggle to shed old clothes (we see him in various garbs in the trilogy) for new ones, give up one education for another. In fact, his development in the trilogy will be governed by "what he casts off, in terms both of people and attitudes."[8]

This scene is followed by one in which he lies on his bed, with Sarbojaya asking him why he's sulking—Is he missing Benaras? Nischindipur? If he does well as a priest, she tells him, they'll have nothing to worry about. However, Apu's concerns are not with the past, but with the present. With a sudden movement he turns, puts his chin on her lap, and declares that he wants to go to school. This abrupt switch from brooding silence to action defines his pent-up energy, his desire to break into the future. By refusing to provide a rationale, Ray suggests Apu's decision is a compound of many things, perhaps the most important being an intuitive awareness of what is good for him. Priesthood, he can sense, lacks the dynamic for inner growth. Thus there is no putting together of issues in a rational mode. Instead, Apu's choice evolves out of a blend in which thought, emotion, and memory coexist. The most important choices for Ray arise from such blends.

Ray adds another component—a vital one—to qualify the emotion of the moment. Sarbojaya wants to know whether going to school will cost money. Apu responds with, "Don't you have any money?" It's the first juxtaposition of idealism with economics, a relationship that Apu is too young to comprehend. Dreams, Apu finds out as he grows older, come with a price tag, but that doesn't deter him from engaging with them. It is Sarbojaya who makes this dream—his very first—happen by paying for his education with the money she has saved. Throughout the scene we are very conscious of the lantern placed strategically near Apu's head. This is the first appearance of the lantern and its light, which Ray associates primarily with reason and learning. Also during the scene he introduces the sound of the train to suggest a correspondence between Apu's ambitions and the larger world of the city where it will take him. Almost subliminally, lantern and train become factors that shape Apu's decision.

In the scene at school that follows, Apu makes a big impact on the inspector, who has come on a visit, when he recites a poem by Satyendranath Datta entitled "The Land of Bengal." This deeply patriotic work, which eloquently describes the glories of rural Bengal, has strong nationalist overtones. The sequence, shot mostly in long take, with the camera frontally framing Apu, affirms a simple but crucial fact—Apu *belongs* to the land of Bengal. The Nehruvian ideal is invoked again: To be truly modern one must first demonstrate his links to his culture. Apu, as he recites the poem with passion and feeling, turns it into his own paean to the place that has nurtured him. He authors his own identity through it (we hear the *Pather Panchali* theme on the soundtrack). But we can only cautiously endorse such an immersion in romantic nostalgia. The fact remains that Apu describes a Bengal that is comprised of words, which is, in short, only a linguistic construct. And we cannot forget that an entire generation grew up believing in this Bengal, only to see it split apart by drought, famine, partition, and communal riots.

The scene acquires other layers of meaning as we notice that it is an all-male class and that everything occurs within a male context. Male sanction is crucial for Apu's evolving sense of self-esteem; in fact, it legitimizes his growth into an adult. This will be further apparent when he studies science and English—both male subjects. At home Apu receives sanction from women who nurture him, but in his educational and professional life males dictate the criteria for self-definition. In the shots of Apu studying at Calcutta, we will be treated to the same spectacle of an all-male classroom.

The school headmaster, made proud by Apu's performance before the inspector, takes an interest in his progress. Apu will have to improve his English, he tells him, and then loans him books that together constitute a compendium of a liberal, progressive education: Livingstone's travels; a book on the North Pole; and one on the great men of science—Archimedes, Galileo, Newton, and Faraday. The emphasis on English, science, and geography is a vindication of the values of the Bengali Renaissance, which are also the values of Nehru's modern India. This is what Apu needs in order to supplement his regionalism and embody the qualities of a truly Nehruvian citizen. Thus the two scenes—Apu's reading of the poem and his receiving books from the headmaster—are placed back to back to emphasize the importance of forging a synthesis. Ray wants us to acknowledge the fact that it is *village India* that becomes the site for Apu's negotiations with the modern; even the impulse for education sprouts here.

The headmaster puts it succinctly:"We may live in a remote corner of Bengal, but that does not mean our outlook should be narrow." A Hindu who has converted to Christianity, he is the perfect example of an East–West fusion (he peppers his Bengali with English words and phrases, something Apu will also learn to do). While he looks every inch the rural Bengal schoolmaster, his sense of space is truly global. As the archetypal modernizer of village India, he is a living embodiment of the Nehru–Tagorean dream of blending home and world. His faith in rational secularism and a syncretic culture wins him a disciple in Apu.

Three short scenes follow that demonstrate how well Apu internalizes what he studies. Each scene also redefines his sense of wonder. If in the past such wonder stemmed from a profound phenomenological experience of the world, now it is a wonder determined by scientific principles. We see how nature, even after it is dissected in Apu's makeshift lab, still retains its magic and mystery for him, proving that he hasn't lost his innate capacity for marveling.

In the first scene we see him with a pitcher of water and a small pot. By dipping one end of a rubber tube in the pitcher and sucking at the other end, he siphons the water into the pot. This new epiphany is accompanied by a burst of music, but it is incomplete unless it is acknowledged. Apu's need for a spectator is fulfilled by his uncomprehending mother, who watches her son fashion a new self out of his discoveries. Similarly, in the next scene, with a pair of fruits, Apu explains a lunar eclipse to her. While the lantern serves as the sun, the fruits constitute, respectively, the earth and the moon. There is in such a moment a wonderful sense of the cosmos being present in its smallest and most mundane manifestations, which recalls Ray's remark that the universe is contained within the convexity of a dewdrop.[9]

The third scene transports Apu to a make-believe Africa. Sarbojaya is startled when the door opens with a crash and Apu in a grass skirt, carrying a toy shield and spear, his hands and face dyed black, leaps out yelling "Africa." He jumps around in the courtyard, then runs out through the back door. The scene recalls Apu in his priest's clothes looking at the schoolboys (and takes us even further back to

*Pather Panchali* in which he wore a tinsel crown on his head as he pretended to be a king after watching a folk play). In these successive transformations from Brahmin's son to king, to priest, to "African," Apu traverses a huge space–time divide. From Sarbojaya's medium long-shot point of view, he *could* very well be in Africa, since the dusty, parched Bengal landscape looks very African. For a moment, Apu's empathy with his newfound sense of place in an expanding world seems to have bred the ultimate miracle of transposing one reality onto another. The extension of the local into the global is almost a literal fact.

## A Crisis of Accommodation

Years go by; Apu stands second in the district and wins the scholarship to study in Calcutta. But his talk of leaving Sarbojaya for the city elicits anger and protest from her. She, who had watched his baffling encounters with the modern, is now loath to set him free to pursue it. Apu is now faced with his most important challenge: To reconcile his traditional obligations with his personal ambitions. As the only son and surviving child, he is bound by a sense of filial duty to stay with his widowed mother and take care of her. The second half of the film revolves around this crisis of accommodation as Apu tries to respond to the lure of the urban within the context of his larger responsibilities.

The first sign of discord is apparent when Apu breaks the news of his scholarship to Sarbojaya. He holds in his hand the globe his headmaster has given him (it will replace the lamp as a recurring motif in the last section of the film). For her, this alien object is yet another one of Apu's new acquisitions that distances her further from him. She exits the frame without looking at it. In the confrontation that follows, she asks him what would become of her once he leaves—has he thought of that? But Apu is not the model son willing to sacrifice his future for his mother. Instead, he insists on his independence—modern in itself—by putting his life and education before everything else: "Does that mean I can't study? I must carry on being just a priest?" She sees nothing wrong in that, since all his ancestors were priests. But Apu rebels and won't have her dictate his life. When she slaps him, he runs out of the house. As Sarbojaya, brooding, stands framed in the doorway, we see the emblems of Apu's modernity—the globe and the lantern—on the porch near her feet. She knows intuitively that she cannot hold him back from the city. She also knows he needs to go there for his own good. Torn between seeing her son succeed in the world and her need to be with him, she invests in his future. When she goes out to fetch him, we know she is going to give him her consent. When mother and son return together to the house, she shows him the money she saved while she worked as a cook in Benaras. Once again she provides the material foundations for Apu's dream to come true.

The camera captures Apu's exuberant response as he shouts "Hurray!," leaps in front of it, and makes eye contact with us and the camera. Such a profoundly self-conscious gesture becomes an affirmation of his knowledge of forging his own destiny and having it recorded for posterity. It also signals a whole new relationship with us, since the camera will allow us to become, in his mother's absence, the sole witness to his life in the city.

When he returns to the house, he displays the globe again to her. "This is the earth," he explains, "our earth. Can you see these marks? These are countries. And all this blue—it's the sea." Within such a multitudinous place he shows her the small dot that is Calcutta. What emerges from this is a paradoxical sense of expansion and contraction. The world, which has steadily grown in proportion for Apu, now arrives in his home shrunk into a ball within which his world is no more than a pinhead. And yet Apu not only exists inside this little point but, from within, can conceive of the immensity of the earth and the cosmos. As Sarbojaya listens wide-eyed, barely comprehending, we become conscious of the irony inherent in Apu's "This is our earth." Do mother and son really inhabit the same world? Is it really *her* earth that Apu is talking about? As a further irony, we will see Sarbojaya's world shrink to a *point*—and finally to nothingness—after his departure.

This new sense of space and self is complemented by Apu's new sense of time. In fact, the next sequence opens with a dissolve from the globe to a close-up of a sundial Apu has made. It bears the inscription, "Sundial made by A.K. Roy." Time begins for Apu—a time he "invents," thanks to his education—which he celebrates by proclaiming his authorship. The only previous allusion to time in the film occurred when the headmaster reminded his staff that there was only half an hour left for the inspector to arrive. This sense of functional time, which appropriately exists within the school and has no relevance for the village, Apu makes his own. It will govern his life as he sets out for Calcutta, which runs completely on time.

After the shot of the sundial, we hear Apu tell his mother that it is seven-thirty—time for him to get ready for his first journey to the city. Her time, still mapped by the circular movement of the sun, is completely alien to Apu's notion of linearity and movement—a further source of their separation. Alone, longing for Apu, Sarbojaya keeps time only for his return; otherwise, she lives within the hushed timelessness of the village. The passage of the train in long shot—a moving line on the horizon—becomes a symbolic clock hand that determines his going and coming. Associated with the city, it evokes for her his presence within his absence. And there is also the sundial, another reminder of Apu and his time.

Of Apu's education in Calcutta, Ray provides us with a richly nuanced montage. Shots of professors teaching English and math are followed by those of a test tube, burner, and magnet as Apu continues his experiments. A sense of routine surfaces that was entirely absent in the village scenes as we see Apu in class, working at a press, and chatting with a friend on the riverbank. His daily encounters with that magical entity called "knowledge" have become part of his everyday life, now constituted by subjects within a curriculum. His eagerness to learn remains, but the original sense of wonder seems to have waned under the rigors of a university education.

In this closing section of *Aparajito*, Ray gradually shifts the emphasis away from the nature of Apu's education to the effect it has on mother and son as they begin to drift apart. Apu's neglect seems all the more callous because Ray represents Sarbojaya in a role only too familiar to Bengalis (and that is also a staple of popular Bengali cinema): The self-sacrificing mother, who always places her family before her own interests. If the dutiful son is expected to reciprocate such devotion, Apu seems incapable of it. After he returns from his first visit to Calcutta, we see him on his bed absorbed in his book while she sits apart, sewing. She plies him with questions about the city, then confides in him about how she has not been keeping well: "Will you arrange for my treatment, with the money you will earn?" She doesn't get an answer because Apu has dropped off to sleep. Later, we see him make tentative attempts to measure up to her expectations, but each trip home only serves to bring out his boredom and sense of alienation. Finally, as his visits dwindle along with his letters, we sense his failure in trying to bridge two different worlds.

Just before Sarbojaya dies Ray opens with a shot of the sundial, then cuts to a tree at whose base she sits, deathly ill. When she hears the train, she opens her eyes. We see her poised between two different time frames: The organic as embodied by the tree, and the functional as represented by Apu's emblems of train and sundial. It is to the latter that both mother and son lose out, for even the train cannot get Apu back to the village in time to be with her. As she dies alone, deprived of the traditional comforts of family and community, her death acquires a sense of closure, bringing to an end an entire way of life. For Ray, all change inevitably involves some form of sacrifice; Sarbojaya's death is the price Apu must pay on behalf of progress. To have compromised his future by staying back in the village would have been equally tragic for him. We are left, then, with a sense that destruction is necessary for creation, that "the two forces [are] eternally interlinked."[10]

Ray conveys this feeling very sensitively as Apu finally reaches home and pours out his grief. As he sits under a tree and weeps, the

camera discreetly tracks back and leaves an open space in the foreground of the image. It becomes a visual equivalent of the freedom
and emptiness her death generates for him, and it serves to balance
his sense of guilt and sorrow. We last see him walking toward the railway station to catch his train to Calcutta. Free now to pursue his life
in the city, Apu doesn't look back, not even once. As we hear thunder on the soundtrack, the camera tilts upwards to show the sky—
another metaphor of open space; in this case, limitless space. Apu's
choice of pushing forward on his path, "rejecting hindrances which
serve no useful purpose,"[11] already displays a new consciousness
aligned to the rhythms of the city. The boy, who sat on the porch
holding his slate, is now ready to inscribe the world on it.

## Notes

1. Chidananda Das Gupta, *The Cinema of Satyajit Ray* (New Delhi:
National Book Trust, 1994), 35.

2. Ibid., 33.

3. Robin Wood, *The Apu Trilogy* (New York: Praeger, 1971), 20.

4. John Russell Taylor, "Satyajit Ray," in *Cinema: A Critical Dictionary*, Vol.
II, ed. Richard Roud (London: Secker and Warburg, 1980), 815.

5. Wood, *The Apu Trilogy*, 51.

6. Ben Nyce, *Satyajit Ray: A Study of His Films* (New York: Praeger,
1988), 13.

7. Ibid., 13.

8. Wood, *The Apu Trilogy*, 45.

9. Folke Issakson, "Conversation with Satyajit Ray." *Sight and Sound* 39,
no. 3 (1970): 120.

10. Wood, *The Apu Trilogy*, 57.

11. Ibid., 58.

*two*

# The Apu Trilogy:
# Apu's Other Education

**E**ven as we see Apu in school and college, we sense his other education going on simultaneously. For Ray, the growth of Apu's subjectivity depends as much, if not more, on how well he responds to the experience of daily living. The trilogy repeatedly focuses on the new integration of experiences, some of which are almost subliminal in nature. Ray prefers to insinuate change rather than proclaim it through a set of contrived situations. Some of Apu's most profound moments of discovery occur within the everyday, often in circumstances that are deliberately underplayed. This is true even when Ray focuses on specific experiences like death or grief. His purpose is not merely to define a particular event in Apu's life, but to show *how* it shapes a personal response. We become conscious of a complex inner process at work as Apu grapples with his father's absence, solitude in the city, his sudden marriage, and the pain of multiple bereavements. It is the corresponding growth in subjectivity that Ray wants us to explore. Although he will occasionally identify some of Apu's choices as "modern," the modernity of the trilogy lies elsewhere. It is most felt in Ray's ability to emphasize Apu's consciousness as a subject in itself and to involve us directly in its extraordinary evolution.

### Family and Solitude

The sense of solidarity Ray suggests in *Pather Panchali* as Apu writes on his slate surrounded by his family soon proves quite illusory. Within a patriarchal rural community the husband, who provides for his wife and children, is responsible for their well-being. The task of ensuring the stability and cohesiveness of the family rests on his shoulders. Harihar, in *Pather Panchali*, seems hardly an authority fig-ure, "absent even when he's present."[1] Idealistic and impractical, he dreams of being a successful poet-playwright while his children go hungry, debts pile up, and the house is almost coming down on their heads. Even worse, he stays away for months looking for work, not even remotely concerned with how the family will fend for itself. We learn from Sarbojaya that this is not his first "desertion"—he spent eight years in Benaras after their marriage, leaving her with her parents, not bothering to write even once. Thus Harihar is proven to be an entirely ineffectual male, unable to fulfill his traditional patri-archal obligations toward his dependents. Although Ray does not turn him into a villain, there is a tacit criticism of the educated priestly class corrupted by pride, ego, and power.

The only activities we see Harihar engage in are writing, teach-ing Apu, eating, praying to the gods, and reading from the scriptures to the widows (in *Aparajito*). On the other hand, Sarbojaya is associ-ated throughout the films with grinding manual work. In fact, it's hard to think of a single scene where she's not *doing* something. She not only performs her womanly duties centered around the kitchen, but also takes on traditional masculine functions: defending Durga from slander, worrying about the survival of the family, urging her husband to act (fix the roof, repair the kitchen), selling utensils to procure rice, working as a cook in Benaras, and providing money for her son's education. While she continues to defer to her husband, we sense an independent spirit that struggles to assert itself. By creating a feminized male and assigning certain male functions to a woman, Ray inverts roles and duties traditionally determined by gender.

Growing up within a patriarchal society that urges him to identify with his father, such inversions cannot but confuse Apu. There are very few scenes in the trilogy in which we see father and son together. In fact, Ray repeatedly emphasizes Harihar's physical absence when his son needs him most. In his moments of profound dislocation, Apu is usually alone (even when he's surrounded by people). The scene that immediately comes to mind is in *Pather Panchali* as he watches Durga being accused of theft by the neighbors, then being beaten by her mother. He is the sole male witness to the event, and the recurrent cutaways to his face suggest not only shock but a painful inability to formulate some form of intervention. Later, during Harihar's protracted "disappearance" from home, his vulnerability intensifies as the family moves closer to starvation. Left alone with his mother on the night Durga dies, then having to fetch the neighbor the next day, Apu has to grapple with an incomprehensible tragedy without his father's mediation. If all this eventually generates an Oedipal revolt, then it is evident in his rejection of priesthood and his departure for the city. And yet there is no real purging of Harihar's presence from his life. There is a tangible sense of son duplicating father—although in very different contexts—as he turns away from his mother and abandons his son. Moreover, in *Apur Sansar*, something of Harihar's irresponsible romanticism is present in Apu the writer, who also dreams of literary fame and confuses art with life. It could be argued that only when he accepts Kajal's urging of responsibility and becomes the kind of parent Harihar could never be to him that Apu finally exorcises his father and "enters full manhood."[2]

In Harihar's absence, Apu, in *Pather Panchali* and *Aparajito*, is associated repeatedly with the women who replace his father. Growing
up among them, he develops quite early a sense of his privileged status as the preferred male child. When Durga catches him stealing her
tinsel and beats him, Sarbojaya immediately intervenes and takes his
side. While such attention is empowering as well as emotionally
deeply nourishing, it encloses Apu within a protracted maternal
embrace. As he grows older, he tires of such self-enclosing love. In
fact, it becomes an unconscious factor in his shift away from his
mother. It is significant that only in Calcutta, away from the maternal village, that Apu can develop his first male friendships of any substance. In Nischindipur or Mansapota we do not see him with a single male friend of his age.

The city, with its emphasis on education, technology, work, and
solitude, becomes reassuringly male for Apu. He also identifies with
its secular space—not once does he allude to his caste to define his
identity, thus separating himself even further from Harihar, the
staunch Brahmin. It is also in the city that he distances himself from
women. His female neighbor in *Apur Sansar* takes an interest in him
but he scrupulously avoids her. We watch him discreetly close the
shutters of his window on her as she stands framed against her window, looking into his room. Such sexual timidity can be traced to his
women-dominated childhood in which any significant contact with
the opposite sex was solely through his mother and sister. Thus it is
only within the imaginary—in the romantic scenarios of his book—
that he can fantasize about the female Other and disarm her threat.
Pulu will point this out to him—what does Apu really know about
love? And how can he write about something he hasn't experienced?
Aparna will be the first woman in his life who is neither a mother
nor sister, but ironically enough for him, she too will reinforce the
notion of the maternal by dying during childbirth.

In addition to these psychological dislocations that Apu experiences within the family (and that includes multiple encounters with
death), there is the trauma of physical displacement that begins with

his uprooting in *Pather Panchali*. For Ray, these displacements and relocations belong to a pattern of migrations that he associates with modernity—with its rootlessness, disruption of community, and reality of solitude. It is in *Aparajito* that the impact of this process is really felt as the family, now living in Benaras, exists without an immediate community, no ancestral plot of land, and no elders to remind them of their roots. Once Harihar dies, Apu and Sarbojaya are thrust into a world of uncertainty as the traditions and values that have sustained them begin to crumble. While she is forced to take on a job as a cook, Apu earns a few coins by plucking grey hair for the old man in the family. He seems destined to become a servant in this household until his mother sees the danger and decides that they should live with her uncle in Mansapota. Still, Mansapota is not their ancestral village, and Apu's attempts to connect with his forefathers by becoming a priest is doomed in a changing world from which his father—the symbol of continuity—is absent. His departure for Calcutta hastens the disintegration of the family that Sarbojaya's death completes. At the end of the film, Apu has truly come to embody the aspirations of a whole generation that migrated from village to city in search of a new life.

When *Apur Sansar* opens, the most conspicuous change in Apu's life is the fact of his solitude. But Ray doesn't portray him as an alienated soul lost in the urban jungle. Apu not only relishes being alone, but is reluctant to give up his independence. When Pulu offers him a job as a clerk, he refuses it. He is happy in his garret of a room, poor but free to nourish his dream of becoming a successful writer. "Why slave away at a desk," he tells Pulu, "when I'm a free man." His books, his flute, his photographs of famous writers on the wall suggest a self-contained and self-enclosed world, but one that is precariously aligned to the rest of the world outside. The sound of the train, which we hear immediately after the film begins and that invades Apu's room at all times of the day, points to the fact that he cannot live isolated from the realities that surround him.

For a man who grew up in an extended family, such evident pleasure in solitude is distinctly modern as well as urban. It is also romantic, shaped substantially by Western education—in particular, the study of romantic literature. Apu feels empowered by the fact that he can overcome the impoverished circumstances of his life through his imagination and creativity—in short, through art. We sense his total commitment to the book he's writing and his conviction that he has it in him to be famous and successful. As he tells Pulu, "Those who have real talent can do anything."

What seems curious is that the boy who showed such enthusiasm for the sciences in *Aparajito* should make literature his abiding passion as an adult. Apu, who dozed in his class on English rhetoric, now relishes the power of the word to invest the make-believe with reality. When we hear him recite Tagore and speak with emotion about Goethe, Dickens, Keats, Lawrence, Dostoevsky—clearly his favorite authors—we sense a dramatic shift in consciousness. From an investment in objective scientific fact Apu has embraced the imaginary that signals a radical reformulation of his notion of reality itself. As he turns increasingly to his feelings, we see how such a shift shapes his response to marriage and love.

## Marriage and Love in the City

For Ray, who always upholds community and the fact of living together, marriage acts as a bulwark against loneliness and isolation. As the priest in *Aparajito* tells Harihar, there is no happiness without a family. He has saved money literally by starving himself so that he can find a young woman, marry, and settle down. While Ray upholds such bonding, he is critical of the institutionalization of marriage within Indian society. Sarbojaya and Harihar's marriage in *Pather Panchali* is defined by the orthodox rural society within which they live. One marries to produce an heir, to maintain continuity, and keep the ancestors happy—all this in keeping with the injunctions of the scriptures. The notion of personal happiness or romantic love is alien to such a marriage that is arranged by the parents often with the help of a middleman. Since a wife must remain subservient to her husband—power relations are unequal from the start.

In *Aparajito* Sarbojaya's neighbor asks her to get Apu married off while he is in the city because "once the bride comes home, all your worries will be over." It is significant that the direct beneficiary of Apu's marriage is not himself but his mother. It is designed to end Sarbojaya's immense loneliness, providing her with a companion as well as help in her day-to-day household activities. It is taken for granted that the wife will live in the village away from her husband while he finishes his studies in Calcutta. After all, a woman not only marries into the groom's family, but marries the family itself.

It is against this pattern of orderly negotiation that Apu's totally arbitrary wedding takes place. Such an "absurd" situation—the guest marrying the bride to save her from ostracism—could be explained in terms of the Hindu notion of fate: Their marriage was destined to be. But the film suggests a more intangible logic: They were fated to marry because they had the potential to find happiness in each other. Such an idea is implicit in Ray's extraordinary tracking shot that connects Apu to his destiny. As Apu lies asleep under a tree, clutching his flute, his head on a book, the camera, seemingly with a will of its own, tracks all the way past the bridegroom's wedding procession in the distance until it finds him. Thus he is subtly linked to the larger pattern of events that, unknown to him, are forming and that forever will change his life.

If marriage in *Pather Panchali* is critiqued for its patriarchal bias and inequalities, *Apur Sansar* attacks its orthodox nature. When Apu finds out that Aparna would be cursed if she didn't find a husband that night, his first reaction is one of shock and disbelief: "Is this a play or a novel? . . . Are you still living in the Dark Ages?" Not only is Aparna helpless within a traditional system that denies her basic rights as a human being, she's also completely at the mercy of her father who had arranged the match and expected her to marry the groom even after he was found to be insane. While Apu's outrage and choice of words at such inhumanity are proof of his modern, rational outlook, it is framed within a self-critique. By challenging the irrational practices and patriarchal foundations of the rural world, Apu is exorcising the demons of his own past. In the process, he measures his growth away from the "primitive" village.

But such indignation at first seems only a matter of rhetoric. When he is asked to rescue Aparna by marrying her, he turns down the request. Only later, alone by the river, we see him change his mind. Ray does not attribute his choice to a simple triumph of reason or humanitarianism; in fact, he never explains precisely what causes Apu's turnaround. We sense a whole complex of factors at work: Compassion for the abandoned woman, memories of his own dislocations, a certain naive heroism (he will later tell Aparna that he thought he was doing something "noble"), as well as the wail of an unidentified child that serves as "an emblem of vulnerability."[3] As with Apu's decision to go to school, there is a sense of an entire life shaping an action.[4] Perhaps the most important fact that emerges is that he *makes* a choice. Moreover, there is a sense that Apu, who resisted the idea of marriage only minutes ago, has perhaps realized that to protest a socioreligious practice does not truly express a modern attitude—it has to be backed by action. And by agreeing to marry Aparna, he performs a profoundly moral act.

The next phase of the film, set in Calcutta, serves as a study of a marriage in an industrialized urban setting where love must contend with poverty, squalor, and the endless screech of train whistles. In the absence of an extended family, the couple enjoy the rare privilege of unlimited privacy and independence—a fact that Ray underlines repeatedly. It suggests the uniqueness of their marriage, which will be confirmed in other respects as well. But while their absorption in each other is necessary for the happiness they experience, it can also fatally block them from any significant contact with the world outside. Sure enough, the city seems to recede from them spatially, visible only through windows or in long or medium shots. We never see them inhabiting urban space except within enclosures such as a carriage or movie theater, which only serves to insulate them. At the same time, we are never allowed to forget the city's highly invasive presence—especially through the symbolism of the train (at one point Aparna covers her ears from its terrible scream).

We have already noticed the grim environs in which Apu lives: the shanties by the tracks, the shabby streets, and even shabbier buildings nearby. And we know the hard facts of survival: strikes, unemployment, the pittance Apu earns from his job as a clerk, and the private tutorings that keep them from going under. But such realities cannot blunt what is precious and enduring between the couple. Here lies the key to Ray's romanticism in the film: The harshness of the environment acts as a foil to emphasize their sense of contentment. Love thrives despite the factory chimneys and smoke-belching locomotives. As Apu's fellow clerk asks: "Why don't you tell me your secret? How to be happy in these hard times, with a wife and a job that pays forty-five rupees a month?" A casualty of love in the city, he is saddled with a bland wife and an insufferably dull marriage. And he resignedly brandishes a milk bottle. This is the sort of marriage against which Apu's own marriage holds ground, proving how two people thrown up against each other by chance can find happiness and love through mutual self-respect, affection, and interdependence. For Ray, the modernity of such a marriage lies in this spirit of reciprocity, how it is shaped and sustained by individual sensibilities. Although we never see Aparna with a woman her age, she never complains (as Sarbojaya does in *Pather Panchali*) of not having someone to confide in. Apu is not simply her husband, but her best friend. The justly famous morning-after scene describes this reciprocity, but it also draws attention to certain broad inequalities that nevertheless exist within the marriage. However enlightened Apu may seem, we find he is still dogged by his patriarchal legacy.

The scene opens with the sound of the alarm clock. Apu has knotted the end of Aparna's sari to his sheet so that when she gets up, she's pulled back. She unties the knot, slaps him playfully on the back, then goes out of the room. Ray cuts to a shot of Apu opening his eyes and slowly turning his face toward the door, then lifting a hairpin from near his pillow. He looks at it dreamily, then, head back on the pillow, watches Aparna as she prepares the oven. She senses his gaze, looks at him, smiles, goes back to work, then asks what he's staring at: "Am I new here?" Apu doesn't reply but takes out a pack of cigarettes from under his pillow and discovers Aparna's note inside, reminding him of his promise to smoke only one after each meal. He puts the pack back under the pillow and his glance collides with hers. We continue to watch Aparna from his point of view as she goes to the coal bin on the terrace. Recoiling at the sight of a cockroach, she squashes it with a broom. She then squats on her haunches and begins to break the chunks of coal.

The scene plays out at first as a discovery scene—what it is like for a man who has been sexually timid all his life to wake up in the morning in his old bachelor's bed and find a woman sharing it. We notice the small changes in the room: The new curtain replacing Apu's torn one, the potted plant on the window sill, the primitive portable kitchen now out on the roof—all of which point to a woman's hand at work. But the changes that affect Apu the most are articulated through look, gesture, and the use of details. The hairpin, for example, could never have been there before, nor was there any-one to stop Apu from smoking. These apparently insignificant facts are singled out and given a powerful evocative presence.

The alarm clock signals the start of a new day in the big city. And we hear the trains outside at once. Ray links time to movement, to machines, to technology, which all figure, directly or indirectly, in Apu's life. But for her, waking up in the morning means preparing the oven, breaking coal, and cooking a meal for him before he sets off to work. Ray doesn't spare us the details: The coal dust on Aparna's hands, the cramped space within which she has to work, how she lights the fire, fans the flames, kills the cockroach. We see everything through Apu's eyes. Like Harihar, who would not have thought twice of Sarbojaya's doing her chores as housewife, Apu, at first, seems to succumb to the same callousness.

We sense the disparity of roles primarily through Ray's high-lighting of body language and his use of the gaze. Apu, lounging in bed and looking at his wife adoringly, may seem to be the fond lover, but it is also a male posture that conveys self-indulgence. Moreover, his gaze is a possessive and self-empowering one. She is *his* wife and it is *his* life she has enriched; he can thus afford to lie in bed, yawn happily, and feel he is entitled to his gaze and having it reciprocated. But Apu is far too sensitive to surrender to such a vision of "cosy" domesticity. The scene literally serves as an eye-opener as he reformulates his male gaze to truly *see* her. She is transformed immediately into a woman hunched over, breaking chunks of coal, no different from a hired maid.

In the scene that follows, Apu comes out of his room playing on his flute but stops and watches Aparna. She carries on with her job, pouring a trayfull of coal chips into the oven, then carrying it past him further down the terrace. While she is all movement, he remains a silent brooding presence, seemingly incapable of intervention. But Apu's actions, we know, are always preceded by moments of deep introspection in which he seems to stand apart from the world that surrounds him. In this case, he breaks out of his reverie by putting on his slippers and announcing that he's going out to find a maid. But she stops him, sits down next to him on the bed, and puts her chin on his shoulder. Thus framed within Ray's medium close-up, their togetherness is defined as an antidote to all ills—social or economic. Apu does nothing more to remedy the situation but simply accepts his wife's plea not to bother about her. She can manage everything as long as he is with her.

Such an acceptance of a woman's drudgery in the name of love seems much too complacent. Apu seems incapable of the sort of moral action that he displayed when he decided to marry Aparna. In this respect he is very much the traditional Bengali male who aspires to be modern, but is culturally too inhibited to formulate a radical stance. The next sequence, designed to reaffirm their mutual fondness, contains a shot of Aparna fanning Apu while he eats, followed by a shot of him fanning her while she eats. Thus equality is restored—or so it seems. Apu's anguish over coal-blackened hands, gender roles, and gender discriminations has faded as quickly as it surfaced. In the very next scene he asserts his male superiority as he teaches Aparna English.

The subject of her education comes up as early as their wedding night. When he learns from her that Pulu has told her about his novel, he asks her whether she can read. Although the question has more to do with his ego than with her literacy, it nevertheless reveals what he values in a woman. When he finds out that she knows Bengali, it is clearly not enough for him. The shot of Apu teaching her English points not only to a woman's education by a man, but also points to an education on *his* terms, according to what he thinks is good for her. While such a lesson may suggest his need to make her his equal, the only English word she utters in the entire film is, significantly, "wife." The whole point of the project, it seems, is to make her define herself in relation to him. And that too in a language that is linked to his sense of empowerment, because he has mastered it.

The scene in which she claims to be his spouse is also the scene in which Apu describes to her the worth of his book. He tells the pregnant Aparna that while she is away at her parent's home, he will have a go at the novel that he hasn't touched since their marriage. His love for her, he affirms, is much more meaningful than everything else he does, including write. The book, a relic of his solitude, holds no attraction for him when she is with him. Only in her absence can he return to his old passion. By placing her at the top of his hierarchy of value, where she replaces his book, Apu displays the symptoms of a fatal obsession. We have already noticed the extent of their self-absorption and withdrawal from the real world. Now, by putting her before everything else in his life, he dooms himself to the devastation he will experience when her absence becomes permanent. Faced with her death, his book also will die.

## Death, Wonder, Absence

Aparna's death is one of the five deaths in the trilogy that serve as key formative experiences in Apu's life. In contrast to mainstream Indian cinema, which bristles with melodramatic deaths and an excessive indulgence in emotion, Ray offers highly understated, poetic meditations. Death is conceptualized in the context of other fully formed (and lived) experiences so that it acquires a distinct identity. Its significance is not trivialized by aligning it with a predictable emotion or certain specific emotional displays. Instead, the experience is made concrete and palpable for the victim as well as for those who are directly affected by it.

Placed within a living continuum where it is linked to the life-affirming processes of renewal and continuity, death becomes, by qualification, an essential element of life itself. Nothing really ends with death, but becomes absorbed into other things. For the living, the long-term experience of loss often proves transformative as it deepens their sensitivity and generates a more complex awareness of life. In fact, there is a sense of compensation for each death in the trilogy. As Robin Wood explains: "Loss is usually accompanied by gain, and each death leads, either immediately or indirectly, to progress."[5] Underlying such an attitude is Ray's notion that life is a complex, inclusive whole made up of diverse experiences. Death and life thus cease to be opposites, but function as complements. Both are vital to existence, and one cannot *truly* live without taking into account the fact of death. The key to a fully rounded philosophy of life, as Apu will find out, lies in developing such an awareness.

In *Pather Panchali* Ray juxtaposes Apu and Durga's discovery of Indir's death with their discovery of the train. His purpose is to show how two disparate events generate a dialectical relationship within Apu's mind; in order to recall one he would inevitably have to recall the other. Both experiences are incomprehensible for him at his age, but they acquire an epiphanic dimension since they are linked to his sense of wonder. Ray suggests that years later when they become mere facts they will retain something of the mystery they hold for him now. But more important is Apu's burgeoning awareness that life is full of dualities that coexist within a unified, interrelated pattern.

Ray sets the train scene in a field of *kaash* flowers that dwarf Apu. The tall grasses, the flowers, the buffaloes in the water, Durga chewing on a sugarcane stick: all these details evoke the rural heart of Bengal, an idyllic pastoral world. But this preindustrial innocence is immediately qualified by the pylons—telegraph poles—that stand in a row. Their mysterious hum baffles the children who listen with their ears to them. Apu's question—"Where are we?"—confirms the feeling that this is indeed a magical world far removed from the familiar.

As Apu and Durga, hearing the sound of the train, run across a field, the train appears on the horizon line above the white flowers. From the shot of Apu running toward it, Ray cuts to a shot of the engine from a fixed low angle. We assume it is from Apu's point of view until the train goes past and we see him on the other side of the tracks. Through a disorienting shift in perspective, Ray discourages us from merely reading the scene in terms of an epiphany. As we see the train cut a swathe through the fields, there is a sense of invasion. It literally "obliterates the landscape and shatters its serenity."[6] Apu, rendered small and frail, is reduced to "insignificance."[7] The sequence ends with an ominous hint of pollution as a black cloud of smoke hangs low over the *kaash*. Suddenly the pylons and the train collide with the traditional Eastern sense of man's oneness with nature. They become symbols of Western technology, of a new concept of progress that is based on man's exploitation of nature. As we witness the preindustrial world succumb to the rule of the machine, our sense of Apu's wonder and enchantment is qualified by a larger political and ecological awareness. Our attempt to balance these conflicting points of view helps us to identify with Apu's struggle in the next scene as he tries to incorporate his experience of the magical train with that of death.

Each death in *Pather Panchali* and *Aparajito* invariably evokes nature. Indir dies within a bamboo grove brimming with life; Durga on the night of a severe storm; there is a jump cut from Harihar dying to a flock of pigeons taking flight; and the last time we see Sarbojaya, she is associated with a tree, a pond, and fireflies—vital elements that nurture her. While in each case there is a sense of a transformation, of an absorption into the cycles and processes of nature, it is Indir's death that evokes this feeling most profoundly.

As she sits hunched over, deathly ill, wheezing, we hear the sound of the wind and the creaking of bamboo stems in the grove. While she occupies the foreground of the image, Ray's extended tracking shot links her to Apu and Durga who play in the rear. Stealing upon her, watched by Apu, Durga shakes Indir. As the old woman rolls over and her head hits the ground with a loud thud, Ray cuts to a reaction shot of Apu. Disoriented, Durga turns away, accidentally dislodging Indir's tumbler, which rolls down into a patch of water. As the children leave, we see Apu dragging a calf on a rope (it had strayed and they were looking for it).

Here also, as in the train scene, there is at first a sense of different worlds colliding: One alive and flourishing, the other dying; one new, the other old; one dynamic, the other stuck in its fixity. But, finally, Indir's death is nullified by the sheer abundance of life. Her extinction within an ever-replenishing nature only serves to place in sharp relief the deathlessness of life itself. Ray's use of details such as the tumbler falling with a splash into the water and the calf straining at the rope enforces the idea of life as an ongoing movement that is unstoppable. In death, Indir simply becomes part of that process.

We later see Apu and Durga on the porch (which we've come to identify with Indir) while her song plays on the soundtrack. The dog, associated with her when she left home for the last time, stands in the rear of the image. Very discreetly, Ray suggests absence through presence. Indir's porch, her belongings—the material facts of her existence—evoke her presence in the midst of her physical disappearance. At the same time, there is a corresponding sense of others taking over, filling her space. This is Apu's first experience of such absence, but he is too young to translate it into a sense of loss. From Durga's reactions and those of his parents, such absence acquires an emotional color. Ray ends the sequence with the suggestion that Indir will live on in his memory—as the song implies— and that the full impact of her death will register later. For the moment, she has become another enigma, like the train, in a baffling and wonder-filled universe.

Apu is 10 years old when Harihar dies in Benaras and 17 when his mother dies in Mansapota. Both deaths evoke a complex, ambivalent response that contrasts sharply with his reactions to Durga's and Aparna's deaths. Ray shows the father dying in a graphic close-up of his face from the point of view of Apu and Sarbojaya at his bedside. If the explicitness of the shot, which brings it close to melodrama, conveys Apu's dislocation, there is no subsequent display of shock or grief. If anything, Harihar's death serves to confirm Apu's distance from his father, his inability to mourn him. In fact, he speaks of him only once—to Aparna—in the rest of the trilogy. Significantly, it is a reference to his death. On the other hand, Durga's death in *Pather Panchali* leaves Apu with a deep sense of loss. And Aparna's death, in the last film, will bring him close to self-annihilation.

Prior to Durga's death, Ray describes a quasi-erotic and joyous event as she gives herself up to the pleasure of a soak in the monsoon downpour. Apu, shivering in the cold under a tree, watches her. Later, wrapping him with the end of her *sari*, she holds him close to her breast. For Apu, the two Durgas—one utterly vital, the other, later, inert and silent, "asleep" in his mother's lap—will remain forever fused in his memory. Once again we sense a relationship between two antithetical experiences shaping an attitude to life. Apu is too young to rationalize any of this, but there is already a storing away of such moments within his consciousness that will later determine his sensitivity as writer as well as husband and father.

The immediate effects of Durga's death on Apu are carefully detailed by Ray. In the absence of his father, there is none to turn to except his mother, but the utterly distraught Sarbojaya cannot help him. As we see him carry out his daily rituals—brushing his teeth, combing his hair—we recall Durga, who was associated with such activities in the first half of the film. Now, as he brushes his teeth, Apu pauses and becomes distracted. Later, we see him come home alone from his bath; then wrapping a shawl around him, looking suddenly grown-up, he goes off with an umbrella, presumably to school, along the same path that he had traversed with his sister. While Durga has disappeared forever from his world, the spaces she inhabited remain unchanged and as impersonal as before.

When Harihar finally returns home and learns of the tragedy, he cries out in anguish. We have a shot of Apu outside on the road, standing motionless, registering the cry impassively. Durga's death, for the first time, introduces him to loss as more than merely a fact of physical absence. It acquires a palpable *emotional* reality. Although we never see him even shed a tear, he participates silently within the emotion displayed by others.

Ray brings Durga back into the film shortly before the family leaves Nischindipur forever. Hidden away in an old worn-out coconut shell, Apu discovers the bead necklace she had denied having stolen. As he reaches for it, we hear on the soundtrack Harihar tell the village elders that someday Apu will perhaps return to his village. Apu will indeed return in memory to these places, which will never lose their significance for him. Such an allusion to memory acquires a concrete shape as Apu flings the necklace into a pond and watches the water weeds part and then close over the gap, until only a small hole remains. Apu thus consigns Durga's secret into the pond *and* within his memory. It is a tacit way of acknowledging that Durga will always be part of him. It follows from this that perhaps the most important fact about death in the trilogy is how it lives on in others, nourished by thought, memory, and feeling. By often keeping the actual moment of death off screen and focusing, instead, on the survivor's response, Ray shows how death, as a vital experience, makes people live more intensely. This is true even when such responses remain muted and repressed. We are reminded repeatedly of this paradox in the trilogy as we see Apu evolve through grief and sorrow toward self-knowledge and transcendence.

## The Management of Grief

Apu's grief register rises slowly through the trilogy until, in the last film, it peaks. All the sorrow he has kept bottled up within him seems to pour out over Aparna's death. It could be argued that each loss in the trilogy is defined through this bereavement, especially since Apu has been associated with each one of them. In a patriarchal society where it is the lot of women to indulge in emotion, such a display would be condemned as unmanly and certainly not befitting a "modern" man. Apu's prolonged mourning, with its suggestion of self-pity, would appear as a case of misplaced feminine hysteria. Ironically, it is a woman—Apu's neighbor—who tells him to stop grieving and behave like a man; after all, she consoles him, he can easily find another wife.

Apu's challenge in *Apur Sansar*, as we know, is to live life according to his literary blueprint. When he describes his novel to Pulu, we are moved by his idealism but alarmed at his naiveté. The faith he invests in his protagonist makes the latter virtually invincible. Although he struggles daily to survive, nothing can blunt his resolve to get on with life. Such a profoundly romantic vision can be partly ascribed to Apu's youth, and partly to his reading. In fact, his plot closely resembles that of a nineteenth-century European *Bildungsroman*—further proof of how much his Western education has shaped him. Where he goes wrong is to confuse fiction with life, words with facts, appearance with reality. As he sets out, book in hand, to author life, he discovers that life has authored him with a vengeance.

The real test is Aparna's death. Distraught by her loss, Apu does what his protagonist would never dream of doing. He spurns his responsibilities and hides from life, thus betraying the very premise of his idealism. But if grief makes him lose control, the film shows how it also finally reconciles him to life. Apu will mature enough at the end to realize how naive his original thesis was. In order to know life, he must live it first. Only *then* can he claim to write his book. Such an awareness, Ray shows, is shaped primarily by the power of suffering. The final section of the film, in fact, becomes an affirmation of the Indian notion of salvation through pain. Apu's ability to *feel* intensely finally shapes the outcome of his journey. Thus Ray once again emphasizes his emotional growth, but not, as we shall see, at the expense of reason.

Like Sarbojaya's death, Aparna's death is not shown. Instead, we have a powerful evocation of its impact on Apu, starting with a zoom to his face as he hears the news from his brother-in-law Murari. Nothing is held back from us: We see the terrible look of agony in every detail before Apu abruptly turns around and strikes him. While some sort of gesture is needed to convey his complete devastation, the act, nevertheless, seems arbitrary and false. Much more convincing are the dissolves of his face as he lies in bed afterwards. They record his movement from shock and denial to acceptance. Later, when he leaves his bed and stands before the mirror, Ray amplifies the sound of the clock in the room so that its loud ticking is heard over a profile shot of Apu until it stops abruptly. In the profound silence that suggests his total withdrawal from the world, Apu stares at his haggard and unshaven face. It is more than a face—a new self fashioned by grief.

In the next scene we see him standing beside the railway tracks, waiting to throw himself under the wheels of the approaching train. Ray opens with an extreme low-angle shot of the tracks, with the train appearing in the distance. He then cuts to a medium close-up of Apu's gaunt face at eye level. The camera next tracks away from him into empty space and stays there while we hear the shrill whistle of the train as it nears. The shot offers a simple yet powerful visual equivalent of Apu's inner void and his desire for oblivion. It is not only ironic that Apu should decide to extinguish his consciousness— once the source of joy and wonder in his life—but that he should choose the train to do the job for him. But the attempt fails when the train runs over a pig that has strayed onto the tracks. Distracted by its shriek, he loses his chance and the train rolls past him. Death, like time, runs out on him, and he is left to convert his death-wish into a need to sustain life. The sequence ends with a shot of an industrial chimney sprouting smoke. We realize that alone in the city Apu is much more prone to suicide than if he had lived within his community, with its sense of traditional values. Urban solitude only exacerbates his pain and lures him toward a death under the wheels of technology. Apu's next move, then, is to sever all ties with the city.

In the letter he now writes to Pulu, Apu informs him of his decision to leave the city. If he completes his book, he will send him the manuscript. He thus invokes the Western stereotype of the wanderer as well as its Indian counterpart, the God-seeking holy man who renounces society out of world-weariness and spiritual longing. Ray puts both together and adds to it Apu's romantic desire to transform suffering through art—through his book. Solitude and art—the romantic's two faithful crutches—are both appropriated by him on this journey "to be free."

In a neat reversal, the train carries Apu away from the city to nature. Renunciation in the modern world, like so much else, depends on services rendered by technology. But as we see Apu on the shores of the ocean and later in the forest, we sense a complete withdrawal from urban life, from its materialism and criteria for success. Cut off from nature, alienated from tradition and community, the city is a spiritual wasteland that cannot offer Apu any solace. Thus, in another neat reversal, Apu rejects the very modernity that lured him away from the village. There is instead a symbolic return to his roots, to nature, to the forest where it all started but where he is now an outsider. The past, Ray shows, cannot be completely relinquished, even for those who think they have broken free from it.

As Apu looks searchingly at the world around him he seems to discover each object with new eyes. Grief has led to a reformulation of the known. When he touches a fern, as if for the first time, we sense a tentative effort to reengage with the consciousness he had tried to kill. There is a harking back to the Apu of *Pather Panchali*, to "the freshness and newness of his childhood" and, in particular, to his sense of wonder.[8] Thus within the ancient spiritual forests of India Apu, now the bearded, deeply introverted seeker, tries to reclaim his lost innocence as well as his primal sight.

The sequence ends with Apu throwing away the pages of his novel, an act that invites multiple readings. Aparna's death has rendered everything absurd, so the book seems to have no more relevance for him. But along with this sense of futility, there is also a realization that words cannot encompass the profundity of his experience. Moreover, life has proven to be far more complex and unpredictable than the writer in him could have ever imagined. His blueprint proved false, the book—and writing—seem a lie. Ray shoots Apu in medium close-up, hands raised, looking dreamily past the camera as the pages flutter away in the wind. The melodramatic framing suggests that his only desire now is to be locked into a deep obsessive relationship with Aparna. If the book stood between them, it's gone. Nothing can stop him from mourning her for the rest of his life.

This becomes immediately apparent when Pulu comes looking for Apu. Five years have gone by since Aparna died, and Apu, working in a colliery, is still in love with grief. As Pulu reminds him of his duty toward his son, Kajal (whom he has never met), and urges him to go back, we sense Apu's refusal to accept any responsibility for the living. The reason he gives is quintessentially romantic: "There's one thing that I can never forget. It's because Kajal exists, that Aparna does not." Grief alone keeps him close to Aparna, a grief that has virtually become an indulgence for its own sake. Even worse, Apu's mourning seems partly directed at himself—as a victim of life's injustices. Thus when Pulu intrudes with his voice of reason, he resists being pulled away from his immersion in self-pity.

If Apu's suffering is to become a redemptive experience, then he needs to end his obsession and redefine his priorities. Pushed beyond certain limits, grief loses its therapeutic, consciousness-forming potential. Apu's emotional gains are threatened unless he can prove his ability, once again, to make a choice—to act positively on behalf of the living. Ray wants some sign, some concrete affirmation without which there can be no regeneration. Apu's decision to return to Kajal and assume his paternal responsibilities becomes that gesture. It marks his rehabilitation in society not only as a caring father but as a sober and rational citizen—"chastened by experience and sobered by self-knowledge."[9] By proving his reasonableness, Apu achieves the crucial balance between head and heart.

For Ray, the father's reunion with his son is particularly significant, because it validates his "belief in the need for togetherness."[10]
Apu's choice ends solitude, dissolves the ego, and promises renewal
and community. Implicit in his reconciliation with Kajal, then, is his
larger reconciliation with life itself. And Kajal, as a symbol of rebirth
and continuity, embodies "the idea that nothing is ever simply
lost."[11] The river, which forms a backdrop to their reunion, suggests
the all-encompassing flow of life. Nothing is indeed lost. If there is
a cumulative truth that Apu gains from the trilogy, then it is to see
life in terms of an all-inclusive unity. Such an awareness is vital to a
fully formed consciousness.

At the end of *Apur Sansar*, as we see Apu walk away with his son
on his shoulders, there's a sense that he too, like the protagonist of
his novel, has stood up successfully to the challenge of living. If the
test of his modernity lay in forming a positive attitude in the face of
change and dislocation, he has shown that he can "confront life's
myriad problems with confidence and fortitude."[12] Will he now
write his book or choose simply to *live*? We never find out.
However, we *are* left with a "book"—the three-part film—that Ray
"writes" for us. As the artist behind the tale who delivers us his complete text and acknowledges our participation in it, he has the last
word in the trilogy.

## Notes

1. John Russell Taylor, "Satyajit Ray," in *Cinema: A Critical Dictionary*, Vol.
II, ed. Richard Roud (London: Secker and Warburg, 1980), 817.

2. Ben Nyce, *Satyajit Ray: A Study of His Films* (New York: Praeger,
1988), 14.

3. Robin Wood, *The Apu Trilogy* (New York: Praeger, 1971), 71.

4. Ibid., 39.

5. Ibid., 16.

6. Ibid., 32.

7. Ibid., 32.

8. Nyce, *Satyajit Ray*, 29.

9. Wimal Dissanayake, "Art, Vision, and Culture: Satyajit Ray's Apu

Trilogy Revisited," in *Cinema and Cultural Identity*, ed. Wimal Dissanayake (Lanham, MD: University Press of America, 1988), 99.

10. Russell Taylor, "Satyajit Ray," 819.

11. Wood, *The Apu Trilogy*, 89.

12. Dissanayake, "Art, Vision, and Culture," 99.

*three*

# Charulata:
# A Woman's Eye

**R**ay's concern with male subjectivity would give way to a series of films centered around women, the most successful of which was *Charulata*, which he made in 1964. Based on a novella by Rabindranath Tagore, not only is the film an example of Ray's attempts to formulate a feminist standpoint, but it also serves as a powerful study of nineteenth-century Bengali society on the threshold of change. Set in Calcutta, the film focuses on the historic moment when two adversarial forces—one white, imperial, Christian, the other feudal, orthodox, and Hindu—engaged in a clumsy embrace that would generate the Bengali Renaissance.

## East Meets West

Although the story takes place in 1879, the film looks back to 1835 when British legislation introduced Western education into India. Since the country could not be ruled unless the ruler could communicate with his subjects, schools and colleges were set up in which English was the medium of instruction. Such a move was vigorously endorsed by Indian liberals such as Raja Rammohan Roy, who felt the study of English could vitalize an insular, orthodox society. But for the British there were other interests at stake. The teaching of English was calculated to impress upon the "natives" the superiority of the master race, so crucial to empire building. It was designed to produce a class of people who, according to historian Thomas Babington Macaulay, would be "Indian in blood and color, but English in taste, in opinions, in morals, and in intellect."[1] Sure enough, such a class did evolve—the *bhadralok*—a bourgeois elite whose exposure to European literature, philosophy, and science bred a profound enthusiasm for the liberal-humanist traditions of the West. Throughout the nineteenth century the *bhadralok* functioned as middlemen, holding administrative posts all over the Empire. It was through their efforts that an uneasy alliance was forged between Western liberalism and traditional Eastern thinking, which brought two disparate cultures together in what is known as the Bengali Renaissance. Roy Armes sums it up succinctly when he writes: "The *bhadralok's* proficiency in English made them the channel through which the new ideas from Europe (democracy, liberalism, nationalism, the liberation of women, and social equality) flowed into Indian society" and spread "an intellectual ferment throughout Bengal."[2]

At the top of the list drawn up by the liberals was the reform of a "backward" society—a reform modeled on the principles of the Enlightenment. Inhumane practices such as widow burning and human sacrifice were abolished; women could go to college like their privileged men; widows could remarry. Soon the drive for "progress" led to an endorsement of most things English. Some Bengalis not only studied the language of the colonizer but dressed in his clothes, ate beef, drank wine, and believed they had surpassed the "Brits" at their own game. And yet under their Victorian outfits they remained Bengalis at heart, living in wallpapered rooms that overlooked their distinctively Indian courtyards. Those who clamored for change were often those who clung most tenaciously to their notion of authenticity within a 5,000-year-old civilization.

In *Charulata*, Ray describes the paradoxes within such a divided culture: Not British and neither Indian as before but a great hybrid built on assimilation and borrowings, on interlocking cultural texts and ideologies. Within such a setup the idea of an imagined authenticity becomes highly problematic. The film shows how culture as an independent, purist entity is no longer tenable in a rapidly transforming world. As the old stabilities and certainties—the old "authenticities"—collapse, the watchdogs of a conservative society that consist of trust, honesty, the work ethic, and fidelity in marriage are all thrown into jeopardy. In a world of fluid, shifting patterns, the "inauthentic" comes to reign. And it becomes inseparable from the sense of the modern.

Ray suggests through his metaphor of shortsightedness that people cannot see very well. They blunder across well-defined boundaries, get their emotions mixed up, violate what is held sacred, and put their trust in issues that backfire. Confusion and misunderstanding are thus rampant in the film. Eager to embrace the new but at the same time tied down to the old, Ray's characters display all the classic symptoms of an identity crisis in their attempt to negotiate with the modern. As they invest in the illusory and confuse it with "truth," their sense of reality becomes precarious. Ray thus repeatedly draws our attention to artifice, to game-playing, to the nuances of writing and language (and the deceptions that are practiced especially through the latter), and finally to cinema itself—the ultimate illusion masquerading as the real.

*Charulata*, then, is also a deeply reflexive film that through specific formal strategies enforces the thematic concern with artifice and illusion. Through its repeated allusions to reading and writing,

weaving and embroidery, newspapers, journals, and novels, it points
to its own creation as a text. Moreover, Ray creates a highly complex system of correspondences "with almost every incident finding
an echo somewhere, down to details of camera movement and
setup."[3] Such cross-referencing extends to all visual elements and
generates an endless process of qualification and requalification that
recalls the structure of music. We become aware of form as *form*,
designed by an artist who proclaims his art-making. And we are
pulled deeper into the film as Ray emphasizes issues that are directly
relevant to us such as spectatorship, the dynamics of vision, and the
erotics of the gaze. Furthermore, technique, which Ray earlier took
pains to conceal, is on display here, calculated to make us reflect on
the fictionality of the work. As if to underscore this even more, Ray
inserts the word "*Nashtanirh*," the title of the source text, onto the
last frame. This final emphasis on writing is a direct reflexive strategy
and another allusion to art and art-making. Thus, in a film in which
the protagonists actively engage in artifice, Ray's insistence that we
see the film as artifact makes perfect sense.

In the film, Charu (short for Charulata) is married to the affluent *bhadralok*, Bhupati, who runs an English-language paper, *The
Sentinel*, which leaves him with no time for her. Sensing her loneliness, he invites her brother, Umapada, and Umapada's wife,
Manda, to live with them, and entrusts him with the finances of the
paper. He also invites his cousin, Amal, who is of Charu's age, and
places him in charge of her "education." Amal, who likes to write,
must coax her into writing herself. Finding no joy in the company
of the dull Manda, Charu turns more and more to Amal until
almost imperceptibly her feelings ripen into love. The narcissistic
Amal quietly eggs her on but lacks the courage to reciprocate her
incestuous overtures. Meanwhile, Umapada swindles Bhupati and
decamps with his money. Amal, afraid of being the source of a second betrayal, leaves one night without informing his hosts. Charu
restrains her emotions but cannot hold them back when his letter
arrives some time later. Bhupati catches her weeping uncontrollably

and guesses the reason. The film ends with a freeze of their hands about to touch.

Given Ray's close identification with the Bengali Renaissance (he has been described as its last representative), one would expect *Charulata* to be a celebration. Instead, he seems eager to critique many of its widely held assumptions. But then, contrary to popular belief, his enthusiasm for the Renaissance has never been unconditional. While he admires its creative accomplishments in music and literature, he has found its typical attitudes to be "superficial, rhetorical and uncreative." The film's questioning spirit may also have something to do with Nehru's death the year the film was made. For Ray's generation it marked the end of a dream shaped by a nineteenth-century cultural ethos. Whatever little remained of Nehru's modern, progressive India would disappear in the flames of political radicalism fanned by the '70s. This was the time to look back and question the idealism that had nourished hopes for nearly two decades. Ray will do this in a full-fledged manner a few years later in the Calcutta trilogy (*Pratidwandi/* *The Adversary*, 1970; *Seemabaddha/Company Limited*, 1971; *Jana Aranya/* *The Middle Man*, 1975); here he examines the very source of the dream and those who dreamed it into existence.

The position Ray seems to take in *Charulata* is that the Renaissance was essentially a bourgeois male fantasy backed by wealth, lofty ideals, self-indulgence, and Anglophilia. Lacking in practical wisdom, it became a casualty of its own high-minded idealism. For the well-intentioned *bhadralok*, the reform of a society was yet another pet project to be mismanaged by their lack of experience of the real world. Most of them, he shows, could not even keep their own house in order. Bhupati, in his Western clothes, spouts the new liberal rhetoric but neglects his wife who remains in seclusion within the *andarmahal* or inner sanctum of the house. He is too busy to notice her bid to break out of her role as a nineteenth-century housewife. He displays "his imperviousness to everything beyond publishing and politics."[5] When the men toast Gladstone's victory in the British general elections, women are denied any participation.

Politics is a man's business just as a woman must raise children and
fulfill family obligations. Women are thus frequently victims of male
insensitivity and thoughtlessness. Amal encourages Charu because
her attentions empower his ego, but when it comes to making a
commitment, he flees. Too weak to dare society or define himself
through a transformative choice, Amal proves that he too is modern
only on the surface but is traditional at the core. For Ray, true liberalism begins at home with men according women the respect,
importance, and equality due them. - English/Indian versus

As he increasingly turns a critical eye on the Renaissance, the
East–West fusion seems just a bizarre set of incongruities that defy
logic. He focuses in particular on the celebration in honor of
Gladstone, since it borders on the unreal. The setting is Bhupati's
wallpapered living room stuffed with heavy Victorian furniture.
Bengali *bhadralok*, dressed in their traditional clothes, loudly extol in
Bengali the virtues of English liberalism before toasting the new
British premier! What is more, we learn that Bhupati's friend, on the
eve of the election, made an offering to the Hindu goddess Kali to
ensure a liberal victory. It is during this display of Renaissance "cosmopolitanism" that Umapada runs off with Bhupati's money, while
in her bedroom Charu seems on the verge of giving herself up to
Amal. Preoccupied with the state of the world, Bhupati is about to
be dethroned in his own home.

Ray also defines a relationship between idealism, Anglophilia,
and language. He shows how the men invent with words a whole
philosophy of living and engage with values and ideals that are far
removed from the realities of everyday existence. Similarly, their
obsession with England is largely linguistic in nature, considering
that most have never been there. In short, we see a culture wholly
seduced by words, unable to define itself through deeds.

Bhupati's amazing prowess with language is on display as he
plays tempter to Amal and tries to make him agree to a marriage
proposal. The bride's father will send his son-in-law to England—a
fact Bhupati shrewdly exploits. He dangles England like a piece of

*Hybridization for desire (26)
of Indian + English
cultures — to weave
it one's own*

bait before his cousin, and it is very much his England—of Burke, Macaulay, and Gladstone—based entirely on his reading. The power of his rhetoric makes it all seem so real that Amal is provoked, in turn, into fantasizing about *his* England—a literary England presided over by Shakespeare. When he dreams of Europe, he naturally conjures up Byron's "Isles of Greece" (he's enamored by the sound of the word "*Mediterranean*," which he compares to the sound of a *sitar*). We watch Amal, the writer, and Bhupati, the political journalist, carve out their respective dream versions of England (which neither has visited). "England" is thus no more than a splendid artifact, packaged in England and disseminated through education to the colonized. First encountered through language, it is reinvented through language again. Such Anglophilia points to a seduction of the mind through words—a key strategy, as we know, within the larger imperial project of colonialism. What is disturbing is that neither man displays any awareness of the politics of language that engages him.) ✓ *English ok.*

## To Be or Not To Be a Nabina

If *Charulata* is a story about the search for the modern, then its real protagonist is Charu and not the confused men who fumble around her. Compared to their overzealous devotion to modernity, she can barely even understand the term or rationalize its nature and function. For Ray, what is of far greater importance is that a woman of her sensitivity and intelligence can *imagine* the modern without giving it a name. From within her *andarmahal* she can sense the changes taking place in the world outside—changes that subtly affect her. Ray seeks to link her story of a woman's awakening to the larger historical transformations that are remolding social and political issues. As Das Gupta remarks, "[s]he is the kind of traditional Indian woman . . . whose inner seismograph catches the vibration waves reaching from outside into her seclusion."[6] We see in her tentative attempts to define herself the aspirations of all Indian women making the difficult transition from the nineteenth to the twentieth century.

In the first seven minutes of the film, which are virtually word-less, Ray describes Charu's solitude and boredom as she spends the long afternoon lounging in bed, embroidering, browsing through books that do not hold her attention, and gazing out of the window through a pair of opera glasses at the diversions of the street. There is a sense that all her afternoons pass this way and that her life is one long routine of endless repetitions.

At first, Ray seems to be pointing to a common female malady in the time frame in which *Charulata* is set. Her boredom, in this respect, is symptomatic of an entire class—more precisely, that of the well-to-do nineteenth-century Bengali housewife satirized by writ-ers as *Prachina* or Conservative Woman who reads pulp fiction, lolls in bed, fusses over her hair in front of the mirror, and thinks only of herself. For a woman who was usually illiterate, with no dealings with the outside world, wholly dependent on her husband, it was easy to succumb to such narcissism and inertia. The culture sanc-tioned it. Most could not even conceptualize boredom, unable to measure it against another way of life or see it as a destroyer of minds. It was a given, a fact of a woman's existence in a man's world. In the film, Manda personifies this condition. She is so inured to her boredom that she doesn't see it as separate from her life.

If Charu at first seems to fit this prototype, our doubts are quickly dispelled as we realize that her boredom is that of a woman who does not like boredom. Moreover, her vital presence becomes apparent even in her walk as she steps outside her bedroom—and inner sanctum (perfectly acceptable at this time of the day since there are no male strangers in the house that she could run into)—to find a book in the living-room cupboard. As the camera tracks with her, the nonverbal and abstract properties of Ray's cinema become apparent. We observe not so much Charu but a moving figure within space that exudes ease and confidence, purpose and vigor, that no *Prachina* could claim for herself. In these first seven minutes, we learn quite emphatically that Charu likes to be on the *move*, to explore spaces that contain her in new configurations. We see her minutes later darting from one win-

dow to another with her opera glasses, following people who like her
are on the move in the street below. We sense her enormous curiosity
about the world as well as her inner restlessness that propels her continuously toward doors and windows. The bed that defines her in sexual and maternal terms (but she is childless) cannot contain her for
long. Throughout the film there is a fascinating dialectic between the
Charu who is sitting inert on the bed and the Charu who is vigorously mobile—the two facets of her personality she seeks to reconcile.

The more we see her in this sequence as well as later in the film,
the more we realize that her boredom in a paradoxical way vitalizes
her—provoking her into thinking, feeling, and, as we will see, creative forms of self-expression. Perhaps even more important, it makes
her dream (largely fueled by her reading) and imagine a life that
could be antithetically different from the one she leads. Ray repeatedly suggests that her solitude, however oppressive it may seem, also
provides her with the freedom to live outside a male-defined universe where she can commune with herself and discover her own
space. In fact, it becomes the only space she has. What she does with
it and within it makes all the difference between being a *Prachina* or
a *Nabina*, or Modern Woman. She must prove—and thus vindicate
Ray's faith in the individual—that she can transcend the limits of her
social condition by virtue of her uniqueness as a person.

Thus Ray seeks to position this elusive self shielded from the
public gaze on film where it emerges deeply and eloquently private.
We are urged to take cognizance of her silence in order to know her
through gesture and movement, through the highly expressive
medium close-ups of her face. What she is not to the world and what
she is to *herself* becomes crucially significant. This shift from the public to a private gendered space violates much of mainstream Indian
cinema where a woman's self is determined in terms of how she
caters to men in the film and male fantasies in the audience.
Moreover, a woman's boredom or solitude is hardly deemed an
appropriate subject for a prolonged cinematic meditation, which is
precisely what Ray engages in.

If Charu then seems poised to become a *Nabina*, the film is built around the question as to whether she will succeed. Or put differently, the film asks what it takes to be a truly modern woman. As we see her within the confines of her "stuffy, brocade-lined cage of a house,"[7] we wonder how well she will be able to assert her presence within the chalked-out limits to her freedom. While her husband is much too civilized to be an abusive tyrant, Charu knows her life in the house is dictated more by the house than anything else. She has not merely married *into* the house, but married *the* house. She knows only too well her place in it.

As a would-be *Nabina* locked inside an old-world system, Charu must negotiate with modernity within a traditional setup. This inhibits her from causing a rupture, from simply rejecting the system or dismantling it. Ray is thus careful not to turn her into a modern-day feminist, but defines her more as an unconscious one who cannot quite comprehend what is driving her forward but who dares social convention through her desires and relationships. Thus, while there is no conscious formulation on her part of concepts such as "freedom," "identity," "rebellion," "infidelity," or "a woman's space," there is a working out of all these issues in her life. Similarly, although she does not plan specific strategies of retaliation against the patriarchy nor engage in an incestuous relationship with Amal to deliver a violent shock, in a sense all of these take place in the film without her conscious intention. Ray's highly understated visual style seems perfectly compatible with "the climate of Victorian reticence"[8] and the understated world of marginalized women in the nineteenth century. Charu's attraction for Amal is conveyed almost entirely through glances, gestures, and the subtlest of nuances that even she misses out on. As John Russell Taylor observes, "[t]he whole story is told in hints and sidelights; in fact, in a very real sense nothing does happen."[9]

*Charulata* then is about a journey of self-discovery that takes a woman into her unconscious. Charu learns who she is in terms of what she has been taught to deny and repress by an over-rigid morality We see her struggle against guilt and fear as she reclaims this "lost" self and brings it to the surface. In this respect, her story encapsulates the experience of all nineteenth-century women who stumble upon their unconscious and turn it into a source of energy and power. The film is perhaps the first sustained study in Indian cinema of a woman's consciousness that seeks to define itself in terms other than those prescribed by her society.

Charu's love of reading and her passion for embroidery become evident shortly after the film starts. Both activities will be emphasized repeatedly. If the former embodies her need for intellectual stimulation, the latter points to the creativity that will burgeon eventually through her writing. Charu's remolding, as we shall see, is indivisibly linked to her creativity. And her love of reading is equally creative in the way it enables her to write herself into a persona. To these creative forms must be added another preoccupation that we have noticed from the start: Charu loves to look—in fact, to gaze, using her opera glasses to draw objects and people up close. We will see how reading, writing, and gazing will provide Charu with the means to intuitively find her way out of the male labyrinth of her time. And they will all converge to shape her most transgressive act: Falling in love outside marriage.

## Redefining the Female Gaze

In a film that emphasizes the lack of self-awareness in people who embrace illusion rather than negotiate with the facts of change, shortsightedness becomes a powerful metaphor. Bhupati sports a pince-nez, Charu has her opera glasses, and at one point Amal looks at Bhupati through a magnifying glass. All three seek clarity of vision, to see objects in their larger details, especially Charu, and yet rarely can they go beyond the surface of things. Training her glasses on the world outside, Charu does not wish to merely satisfy her curiosity but wants her gaze returned, be noticed, achieve contact. But even in close-up, the world remains out of bounds, its proximity only an optical illusion. It invites her to look, but maintains its separateness as the Other. Considering that she is denied entry as a woman makes it all the more significant.

Even within her world, Charu faces rebuff. In the opening sequence, Bhupati, immersed in a book, walks right past her without even registering her presence. When Charu looks at him through her opera glasses, we see him from her point of view, magnified and large, before disappearing down the staircase. He too remains distant, beyond reach. Moreover, he is totally oblivious to the fact that he has been spied upon. As Charu brings down her glasses with a gesture of resignation, we feel her keen sense of alienation. But she doesn't give up. Looking at the world, as she begins to find out, is also a deeply pleasurable activity.

Charu's situation within the bourgeois social setup of the nineteenth century may at first seem paradoxical. While women in their *andarmahal* were shielded from the public male gaze, they were under constant surveillance from those around them. Spied upon by servants and women of the household, any inappropriate behavior was duly reported to the master. While the gazer stayed invisible, his gaze was filtered through other eyes until it could fasten on its object. Although there is no context for such surveillance in *Charulata*, we sense how precarious Charu's privacy is. Once Bhupati invites Amal, Manda, and Umapada to live with them, her space is invaded constantly. And as an unspoken rivalry springs up between her and Manda, both vying to be the object of Amal's gaze, jealousy and mutual suspicion lead to discreet spying.

While a woman's home is deemed a safe haven for her, the film suggests that the opposite is true during a time of great social and political upheaval. The safety issue is based on the assumption that in a patriarchal society women are always at risk from the predatory male gaze. A greater risk perhaps lies in the fact that she could be tempted to reciprocate the gaze—even worse, initiate it. Thus, seclusion from the world is found to be the best solution. Shielded from the gaze and from being desired, she could not desire in turn. In both cases, curbs were placed on the eyes.

*Perception of women in the role in the trad. soc.*

Since at home men knew the bounds of decency within which they could gaze at her, a woman, who mingled daily with her husband's male relatives, had no cause for concern. Although this was essentially a myth, in *Charulata*, whenever the male gaze is directed at Charu, it is never sexually objectifying or threatening. What is more, not even once do the men display any urge to look at her closely through their optical aids, since a woman's presence is taken for granted. In fact, it is more than that. As we shall see, Charu's visibility renders her invisible, especially to her husband. On their part, the men submit to her gaze without ever suspecting that they are being spied upon, since she poses no threat to them. Just as men know the ethical dimensions of the gaze, she too, even more as a woman, must know what constitutes the proper gaze. They can trust her to look and behave with discretion.

Schooled in protocol, Charu does know how a woman should look: Lowered, submissive eyes before elders; the doting look for the husband; the averted gaze before strangers. She also knows that to look boldly, openly, and inquiringly at the world, even worse at men, is a serious violation of propriety. Besides, it impinges on a male prerogative—to possess the world through the gaze.

Charu's gaze thus subverts the norm: Roving, unfocused, pleasure-seeking, fastening itself on objects that have nothing to do with her life or duties, prone to distraction and idle curiosity—even worse, illicit desire. In short, it represents the forbidden look. What is more, it is also the spying, voyeuristic gaze directed at men. But what choice does she have, the film asks? A woman who dares to look outside established decorum must learn to look furtively—to spy. And it is precisely this furtive, secret gaze that marginalized women in a male society adopt and legitimize as their own rightful, "open" way of perceiving the world. Charu's look thus embodies the secret longings of all women proscribed from looking except with a focus and a purpose. Politically, it constitutes an assault from the margins to the center—at those who determine the "correct" gaze.

*how much is Eur. ind. ciy [?]*

Although the inappropriate has no place in the daily optical transactions at home, the film shows that in a world beset with change, it takes very little to turn the "sacred" into the "profane." Such distinctions become meaningless once the system that defined them begins to collapse. No place is safe, no gaze proper or "pure" anymore. In *Charulata*, what seems most subversive is that the woman takes the initiative and not the man. By desiring her own cousin-in-law, she violates that most forbidden of taboos—incest— and initiates a relationship that could plunge a respectable, bourgeois household into scandal. Besides, she proves that she is no longer willing to play the loyal, compliant wife who wants "nothing from life but her husband's happiness."[10]

By highlighting the issue of voyeurism—a woman's voyeurism —which is virtually absent from Indian cinema, Ray initiates a discussion about its nature and function. Male voyeurs litter Indian cinema, but a woman who spies on men? If in a patriarchal society men look at women to objectify them and appease their libidinal urges, Charu's gaze at them does not appear consciously sexual or exploitative. But, at the same time, Ray makes us wonder whether it is merely the curious, inquiring gaze of a woman not allowed to look at men in the eye?

What Charu increasingly discovers is that there is an erotics that underlies all seeing. She can sense her deep sensual pleasure in simply gazing at the world, in running her eyes over the surface of things, but she also discovers that the curious outward glance can become the revealing inward gaze. Thus her shock when her "innocent" pleasure of gazing at Amal turns sexual. She is visibly startled at what her look reveals to her—*of herself*. The act of seeing, then, becomes irrevocably linked to the process of a woman's self-discovery. She finds out what looking is all about and its relationship to desire. Ben Nyce is right when he claims, "*Charulata* is nothing if not a drama of awareness."[11]

Coupled with Charu's outward gaze is the contemplative inner gaze that Ray often juxtaposes to great effect. There are extraordinary close-ups of her face during which we see her stare into space without any apparent focus until we realize it is the gaze within which makes her visible to herself. For example, when Charu tries to write in the second half of the film, or in the opening sequence when she is alone and self-absorbed, she *looks* at herself. But perhaps more revealing are the moments of contemplation that follow her spying on Amal. The erotic is subsumed within the inward gaze and becomes part of Charu's groping toward self-knowledge. Thus the erotic gaze is transformed into the introspective gaze. There is a distinct absence of the will to power or consummation which we associate with the male gaze; instead, Charu, as a female voyeur, combines her solitude, her burgeoning self-consciousness, and her profound sensitivity to *comprehend* what she feels within. Contrary to what one would expect from men, Ray shows how in a woman the erotic gaze initiates a process of rational enquiry and self-reflection.

## Invisible within the Visible

Charu's sense of invisibility, like her solitude and boredom, is a chronic female condition in a patriarchal society, except that she refuses to remain unseen. She is keenly aware that those around her only see her, but never *see* her for what she is as a woman in her own right. Her restructuring of the female gaze—from the focused, proper gaze to the unfocused, curious, spying look—is unconsciously employed to provoke the men in her life to return her gaze, to take notice and render her visible.

The scene in which Bhupati walks past Charu without seeing her is perhaps the most powerful example of her invisibility. Despite his progressive outlook and the fact that he encourages her reading and writing, she has virtually no access to his world and his gaze. He has never bothered to find out who she is, accepting instead the popular stereotype of housewife. Charu must nudge him gently into noticing her by writing and publishing on her own. But these "strategies" bring about no drastic change in Bhupati's vision of his wife. His eyes will only be truly opened when he stumbles upon her infidelity. The discovery scene, although Charu never intends it, becomes in effect her most devastating strategy to make him see.

Unknown to her, Bhupati is a silent witness to her outburst over Amal's letter. Ray zooms in from Bhupati's perspective not only to convey his dislocation, but also the fact that she is caught unawares by his spying gaze. For the first time, as it were, he draws her up close with his eyes. Although he is not wearing his glasses (or perhaps *especially* because he's not wearing them), he can *see* her—as a new woman, unfamiliar, adulterous, even "dangerous." And Charu, without intending it, supremely redefines herself before his gaze. Only such a traumatic event could make him see, and it will transform their relationship forever. Thus there is the paradoxical sense of Charu having also met her match, of losing out to the gaze. The spy is spied upon by the first man who truly returns her gaze. Charu wins and loses.

Similarly, Amal returns Charu's gaze in another crucial scene— except he doesn't even look at her. It is in the garden, freed from the inhibiting house, that Charu trains her "innocent" gaze at him, never expecting it to bounce back at her. As he writes, completely absorbed on a mat, she sits on the nearby swing and indulges in one of her reveries with the opera glasses (we are allowed to participate through point-of-view shots). As her eye wanders to the balcony of the house next door, she discovers a woman holding a child in her arms. Her pause at this inconsequential detail is significant when we remember that she is childless. Ray only allows for a flicker of recognition—the gaze within—before she turns the glasses on Amal, drawing him up where he sits, back turned, quite oblivious of her gaze. Although she displays no sudden emotion we know a connection has been made, that the detail has found a place in a pattern that is unfolding and beginning to disturb her.

Ray, of course, would never claim that Charu rationalizes her sexual attraction for Amal in this way, but merely hints at all the latent possibilities in the gaze. What is most crucial here is her discovery that the unexpected lurks within the commonplace, waiting to subvert self-composure and challenge a prescribed way of seeing. The gaze at the world, she finds out, can hit back hard. In this case, it is returned by the subject who has not even turned his head to look at her. In other words, Amal "gazes" at her more boldly than she could have ever imagined, without even gazing at her.

The next sequence is done in long take and frames Charu's face in close-up. We watch the subtle shifts in emotion that flicker over her face as she struggles with feelings deemed forbidden. We become most conscious of the movement of her eyes, their inner probing—the inner gaze again—as she tries to resolve her conflicting emotions. (The spy finds herself spying on her own feelings.) Faced perhaps for the first time with a crisis, Charu has to think desperately. It is in this thinking, in this communion with self, that she displays her woman's sensibility. The gaze at Amal breeds surprise, worry, introspection, not lust. Aided by her woman's intuition, she formulates a female response. (Looking provides pleasure still, but this time it brings guilt and raises serious ethical and moral questions.) For the first time, Charu has to figure out what she must do with this pleasure: tame it, deny it, disarm its threat? She does not act on it at once as a man would, but contemplates it in silence.

At the end of the film, after Charu has seen through Amal's duplicity and Bhupati has *seen* her, husband and wife meet at the open door. With their eyes truly opened, they can now look at each other without flinching. They seem to have woken up, as Das Gupta puts it, into "the twentieth century, the age of self-consciousness."[12] For Ray, such seeing truly embraces the modern. As for what is inevitably lost, there is compensation in the form of self-knowledge and self-awareness. The freeze of hands that follows describes a pause that is pregnant with possibilities. Within the space of that suspension, Bhupati and Charu must redefine themselves. A series of stills, which come after the freeze and show them poised for contact, enforce the supremacy of the moment. Ray points to the beginning of a new time that will transform lives and usher in a new era. It is imperative that they engage with it, and their reformulated gaze suggests that they are ready.

## The Gaze of the Camera

Right from the film's opening sequence we sense a camera presence that is new to Ray's cinema. As it tracks Charu insistently, looks over her shoulders, approximates her gaze, and frames her through recurring zooms, we become intensely aware of its independence as well as its intrusive nature. If in the Apu trilogy the camera was discreet to the point of being invisible, it asserts itself repeatedly in a reflexive film like *Charulata* (It becomes a participant in Ray's central discourse on issues such as voyeurism, visual pleasure, and spectatorship.) In fact, all the ambivalences of Charu's position as gazer and being gazed at are encapsulated by the camera as it spies on her and defines her predicament as a woman—always under surveillance but powerless to retaliate. At the same time, it also mimics *her* spying gaze by bringing her up close through the zooms and particularly the telephoto lens (a visual equivalent of her opera glasses). Charu, who thinks she is unobserved like her own subjects, is under the constant gaze of the camera, watched as she watches others. At the same time, her wish to be made visible is fulfilled more than she realizes as she becomes supremely visible to us. In fact, the all-seeing, hyperactive camera eye reveals more of her than she could wish for. If she wanted the world to return her gaze, then it is amply fulfilled. But it also means that her privacy, to which she clings dearly, is taken away from her. (In fact, her privacy becomes a very *public* privacy.)

But while the camera asserts its independence, we, as viewers, find ourselves in complicity with its gaze. There is thus a double vision: (The camera's "objective" eye, and our eye observing Charu.) In our privileged position we feel empowered by the mere fact that we can see her—or rather spy on her—while she cannot. Unlike many reflexive films where a character will look directly at the camera and meet the viewer's gaze, Charu is not allowed to return our look (thus mimicking another situation from her life). She remains trapped within the film as in her society. In this respect, (we become the eye within a patriarchal system that women seek to contest but often fail.)

Such a discourse on seeing invariably makes us reflect on our participation as viewers. Ray is breaking new ground in Indian cinema by instilling such a consciousness within a male audience accustomed to indulging sexual fantasies on screen. Our attempts to sexually objectify Charu are thwarted through his mediation. Like Charu, we rationalize our impulses even as we become conscious of them. We also turn our gaze inward from what seeks to distract us outward. The film exhorts its audience to be morally responsible, to (engage with the film critically, and not consume it mindlessly.)

Ray is then not guilty of adopting the very gaze he seeks to critique. Instead, he seeks to create in his metafilm a visual equivalent of the male gaze while engaged in the very act of deconstructing it. Moreover, the camera's gaze is never exploitative as it may seem at first. Framed frequently in full or medium shots and often in medium close-up, Charu remains a wholesome human presence, never defiled by the sexual gaze of the camera or ruptured into delectable body parts. Instead, she is held up to our view so that we may gauge her thoughts and feelings through her expressive body language. The camera aids us in knowing Charu by serving more as a psychological apparatus.

Moreover, her story—that of a woman's burgeoning consciousness—is not what male voyeurism thrives on. Thus a film that deals with voyeurism also shows how it is not a destructive voyeurism, but one that is critically engaged with its own nature and function. If Charu wanted to be looked at as a person by the two men in her life, the camera urges us to oblige her as well. We are asked to return her gaze with respect, compassion, and understanding. Only then can she become truly visible, be truly seen.

Ray is not simply looking at the nineteenth century from the perspective of the 1960s, but wants us to be fully cognizant of the fact that he is (training a camera lens on a bygone era that has never been placed on film) In other words, we are deeply aware of the nineteenth century being photographed by a twentieth-century invention. The kind of visual intrusion and surveillance he describes is of our time, but already in the 1870s this kind of seeing is beginning to take shape and women will gradually engage in it to end a male hegemony. Charu's spying with opera glasses anticipates the machine eye that will do the job better and bring a new form of empowerment to the sexes. More important, it will radically transform the ethics of viewing. *Charulata* points to the start of an entirely new way of conceiving the world, thanks to Ray's powerful discourse of the camera.

But despite the visibility Ray accords her, Charu remains essentially inaccessible—a woman on film, lacking substance. Here also the camera mimics her own relationship to reality and how her society conceives her. If she seeks to make contact (and fails) by drawing people and objects close to her, the camera does the same with her—it seeks to bring her to us and yet our knowledge remains superficial. (Like Charu's opera glasses that can define the surface of things, never pierce it,) Ray's camera also can never give us the truth about her, but only a celluloid illusion that we are invited to accept as real. For us, knowing Charu must remain an ongoing and inevitably imperfect process, just as her experience of getting to know the world is fraught with frustrations. Thus in a film where people mistake illusion for reality, Ray focuses on our contemporary anxieties about the nature of knowledge, the purpose of art, and the relevance of truth. And he incorporates such issues into a meditation on film and its illusory representation of the world.

## The Politics of Reading

Perhaps no other film by Ray makes so many allusions to writing as does *Charulata*. He not only repeatedly includes literary references but, in a film about art-making and the relationship between art and life, where a variety of written and oral texts proliferate, he emphasizes the act of writing itself as a supreme text-making device. In a culture that has always placed a high value on the literary, language acquires a new function at a time of a major historical shift. Ray shows how in the face of a collapsing reality it provides the means for the construction of the imaginary(Writing people, events, and relationships into existence is a way of negotiating with the illusory,) allowing it to take the place of the real when its existence is in doubt. Given the nature of language, such an investment in artifice becomes relatively simple.

We find out quite early in the film that Amal and Charu's fondness for each other has much to do with their fondness for literature. Both suffer from "the insidious fascination of books."[13] Charu finds strength in the hope that he will see her not merely as a woman of the house but as one "who can hold her own in literary conversation."[14] The first words with which he greets Charu are from a novel by Bankim Chandra Chatterji, the most famous Bengali novelist of the nineteenth century, and his first question to her is whether she has read Bankim's latest book. They not only love to read (she only in Bengali), but also write. He, with a callow romantic's fervor, dreams of literary fame and engages in contrived literary exercises. She can write beautiful letters when her husband is away. As it turns out, they are not simply good with words, but relish them with a passion that borders on the erotic. In a film replete with references to oral pleasure and stimulation (chewing betel nut, eating *samosas*, indulging in word games), words are savored for their own sake. Playing with the heady eroticism of language(Amal and Charu become embroiled in a barely expressed but potent eroticism of gesture, nuance, feeling— a private drama of emotions that she authors with language.)

The other person in the film who relishes words—Bhupati— openly scorns all literary texts as soppy and sentimental. He only reads political tracts and thus cannot even conceive of a romantic scenario being "written" behind his back (he doesn't read Bankim, he confesses to Charu). Ray shows how Bhupati's absorption in language—his rather pedantic pursuit of ideas through words—blinds him to reality just as Amal and Charu are blinded by their literary game-playing. There is a scene in the film in which he reads aloud from his writing and defines "individual greatness" in terms of "energy," "patriotism," "devotion to duty," "self-sacrifice," and "an unflinching regard for truth." Such high-sounding rhetoric comes easy to him, but is almost impossible to translate into reality. Likewise, during the film there is a recurrent use of other English words such as "work," "honesty," and "trust," which all have Bengali verbal equivalents. But stated in English, such values are formulated as *English values* and applied to an Indian context. Bhupati upholds them naively as absolutes and cannot even see how people abuse them right before his eyes. Betrayed by those who work for him, in whom he has invested his trust, he loses out to the values of an alien culture that he has sought to graft on foreign turf through language. Thus like Amal and Charu, Bhupati, who also plays with words, is duped by them in the end.

There is a third agent in this drama of literature and literacy—Manda. Charu's lively intelligence sets her apart from this dull and illiterate woman who doesn't know the joy of words or the complexities of language. The act of writing remains a profound mystery to her. Left out from the impassioned word games between Amal and Charu, she asserts herself through her languorous sensuality. If Charu is drawn to Amal through words, Amal is drawn to Manda by her sheer "wordlessness," which renders her wholly ineffectual as an intellectual threat and instead provides him with a sexual diversion. Rooted to the ground, she is more "real" in a world where people routinely reinvent themselves.

The first serious conversation between Charu and Amal about literature significantly takes place in her bedroom, with her on the bed embroidering a pair of slippers for her husband. We are made very conscious of this giant Victorian contraption in the center of the room on which Amal's three-cornered phallic hat occupies the space between which Bhupati and Charu sleep. Within such a suggestively sexual frame, Amal's "education" of Charu begins with Bankim. They talk about how beautiful his women are—a beauty she claims is too perfect and can exist only between the pages of a book. Amal reacts by looking up and glancing at a framed portrait of her as if to draw an analogy, especially when she complains how Bankim's descriptions make her feel inferior. Very gently, Ray hints at a burgeoning romanticism fed by books and images within a setting far removed from the real world.

We know how books, like opera glasses, are vital to Charu, because they bring the world closer to her. Her preference for a modern writer like Bankim, who is known for his progressive, reform-minded thinking (instead of some author of pulp fiction favored by a *Prachina*), shows a highly discerning mind that can engage with the ideas that are transforming Hindu society. We can also sense her identification with his *Nabinas*: Strong, intelligent, book-reading women who aspire to break free from their patriarchal confines, but often with tragic results. And the emancipation of women is only one among other issues such as widow remarriage, political reform, Western liberalism, and love outside marriage that she encounters in his fiction. It is significant that such encounters are always through language.

As we have seen, Ray suggests that Charu's reading gives her the courage to imagine a different existence. Away from the prying eyes of men, ensconced within the solitude of her afternoons, she has a space in which she can remake herself as a literary *Nabina*. She identifies with Bankim's women to the extent that she wishes to become one of them, to live out their forbidden—often adulterous—dreams and rebellions right to the inevitable tragic denouement. In other words, she wishes to write herself into existence. Such "becoming" is a supremely creative act through which Charu moves closer to self-definition. But she also courts the illusory through her choice. Yet, in an age of borrowings, it seems quite right that she should turn to her books in order to live and love. Life, for Charu, will resemble art—with predictable tragic consequences.

## To Write Into Existence

It is then only appropriate that Charu feels the first stirrings of desire for Amal *as he writes*. It seems more than a coincidence that the man with whom she falls in love is a writer, who, like herself, communes deeply with the imaginary. His very act of writing seems to serve as a catalyst: In a subliminal way it embodies her desire to be created, to seek in life that which can only be dared in fiction. Even more, to see him write makes her aspire to be written into *his* life, to figure in his literary and romantic daydreaming. Charu literally "plans" the whole writing agenda: He must use her notebook, her quill, her ink bottle, and never think of publishing what he writes—it should remain a secret between them. When Amal reads out one of his clichéd, literary essays, Charu tells him: "Enough of river, sky, cloud, and moon." Instead, she urges him to write stories, which becomes a subtle plea to write them both into fiction.

Ray provides a montage of Amal furiously scribbling away to give us some sense of the object of her fascinated gaze. His words pour out onto the pages of the notebook she has bound for him—a pouring forth that is seductive and sexual. Entranced, Charu watches as he is transformed by the act she esteems highly. Thus her dream of romance is born quite appropriately in the garden where she feels liberated from the inhibiting confines of the house and where she can glide back and forth on the swing while Amal indulges in his dreams. As Penelope Houston remarks, "[e]ach character is unconsciously using the other as a feature in his own romantic landscape."[15]

It will be inside the house, within the everyday, that Charu's tragedy of a broken heart—true to fiction to the end—will be enacted. As long as she keeps her dream to herself and hides her feelings behind words the scenario works, but as they threaten to spill over, the literary collides with the real and, as it must, shatters.

When Amal asks her to write about her childhood spent in her village, Charu sees it as a gesture of reciprocity and a display of his interest in her. She thus feels deeply hurt when she finds out it is only a ploy by her "tutor" to appease his "master." After all, for Amal her writing is only "an acceptable female diversion" to be encouraged, but not to be taken seriously.[16] Furthermore, the self-serving Amal rubs salt into her wound by announcing that he will send his work for publication—a blatant breach of their contract. Charu is too naive to see that for Amal, his writing is essentially a form of self-

Language, written word
as eroticism

empowerment and self-love. As he puts it, "[h]e who doesn't understand my writing, doesn't understand me." While he solicits her
attention "to confirm his masculine superiority,"[17] he can be brutally callous to her feelings. When his essay is subsequently accepted
for publication by a literary journal, Charu sets out to write herself.
Thus begins their literary rivalry, a form of game-playing that
inevitably involves language.

Like the scene in the garden where Ray's camera gazed at
Charu's face, Ray places her again under scrutiny to this time
describe the birth of a woman's creative self. The shots of her face
suggest at first intense self-absorption. Charu doesn't simply pick up
her quill and write like Amal in a rush of feeling, but rather she
thinks deeply. There is a groping forward, a weighing of options
before a choice is made. In short, she *thinks* her way to the creative
act—a process that recalls her reaction to her own gaze.

Faced with a blank sheet, Charu is momentarily at a loss. When
she hears a cuckoo in the garden, she thinks she has found her subject—"the call of the cuckoo"—only to replace "call" with "lament"
before completely rejecting all such subjects, which evoke Amal's
vacuous romanticism. The student is beginning to move out of her
tutor's shadow. Charu tears up her efforts. The camera then pans
along the rejected, crumpled balls of paper that line the garden path
to the swing on which she sits, rapt in thought. She stares straight
ahead with her customary, fixed, inward gaze—except it is more
than a thinking eye. She seems deep within a meditative silence, a
trance that enables her to commune with her childhood. A set of
superimpositions over her face shows us what she sees with her
inner eye: River, boats, village fair, merry-go-round, fireworks, an old
woman spinning. Sifting through such remembered moments,
Charu finally finds her subject. She writes "My Village" on the
page—a choice that further distances her from Amal, since it suggests
a preference for realism.

At the same time, we can assume that such a rendition of her
childhood is not merely factual but a deeply sensitive evocation,

shaped by feeling and imagination. There is a delving within, a voyage into the interior that writing is supremely capable of inducing. If Charu sensed through her gaze the deep reaches of her unconscious, writing takes her even deeper into the mysterious realms of self. It becomes an extraordinary journey of discovery. We watch her grow "into awareness and strength."[18] Thus the source of Charu's creativity becomes the point of convergence where thought, memory, and emotion all come together. And as with Amal, Ray also links the act of writing to a giving away of self, to a profound sense of release in which perhaps lies the origin of all art-making.

But Charu's subject, we know, is not her own; it was supplied by Amal. Although she appropriates it through her inner searching, she cannot be entirely free of men, even in her creative space. But when the most reputable literary journal of her day publishes her essay, Charu successfully encroaches on male territory. As she triumphantly points out her name to Amal, we see the word *adhikarini* in the final sentence, which denotes authority and power. She has carved out a new identity for herself, and from being authored in a male world she has become an author in her own right.

When Amal reads the essay and turns to look at her, we sense his new look of respect and admiration. "I've been completely fooled!" he tells her. Bhupati, who is not told, finds out at the musical soiree in honor of Gladstone when a friend displays the essay to him. There is a shot of the men milling around him, peering at the page to see Charu's name—a *woman's* name. Like Amal, Bhupati cannot believe his eyes. Thus she beats her language-obsessed men at their own game and draws them away from language to *see* her truly. Naturally, cleverly, she uses language as her means.

But if Charu seems bent on retaliation, such an intention dissolves in tears. When Amal tells her she must continue to write, she breaks down and weeps on his shoulder, telling him repeatedly that she will never write again. In love with him and unable to restrain her feelings anymore, Charu's rejection of writing is also a symbolic rejection of the literary romance she has initiated. She is tired of

words and hiding behind them, since they cannot disguise her feelings anymore) Now she only wants his love. But even if she wants to
break free from language, she is denied that freedom in a society
where she cannot reveal her "illicit" desire. Thus a little later we find
her playing a word game with Amal that revolves around a particular Bengali alphabet. Throughout the film we have seen them engage
repeatedly in repartee, rhymes, puns, and wordplay (all virtually
impossible to translate into English). Now their last word game,
fraught with suggestive undertones, ends predictably in mutual
embarrassment. Words prove wholly inadequate again as subterfuge.
The scenario has changed dramatically to one of "pent-up emotions
trembling on the verge of open expression." [19] The final rupture with
language will occur a few scenes later when she will clutch Amal's
letter in her hand and pour out her feelings.

But before that happens, Amal sneaks out at night. Next morning, when Charu finds out and runs into his room, Ray zooms from
her perspective to suggest how her eyes have been opened by this
betrayal. It is her moment of truth when she finally *sees* Amal in his
true colors. But she recovers sufficiently to accompany Bhupati on a
holiday by the sea during which he remains oblivious of what has
transpired behind his back. In this new space, away from Amal,
Charu shows a willingness to negotiate with language again. At first,
her proposal to write for his paper draws laughter from him, but she
doesn't give up. She comes up with an even better proposal—a bilingual paper that they will jointly edit: she will take care of the Bengali
section, he, the English. Struck by the originality of her proposition,
he readily approves of this partnership. Charu thus makes new gains
in her quest for visibility. Her maiden writing venture has given her
the confidence to force an even larger entry into a male province.

But just when she thinks she has grown stronger with words, she
flounders. Even unread, Amal's letter in her hand is a live bomb.
Succumbing to the power of invisible words, the inscrutable Charu
finally surrenders to her emotions. And it seems only appropriate
that their relationship that had been inaugurated with words, should

end with them. As a storm blows the window open and she collapses weeping on the bed, all that she had repressed behind words pours out. She, who loved words, proves in the end that she can also express herself as intensely with feeling. In the process she transcends language.

Although Charu's literary romance, inspired by Bankim's novels, draws to its predictable tragic climax, we are left in no doubt as to what she has accomplished as a woman. Her forbidden love, we know, could occur only in a book or play, but she takes it beyond the written page, smack into life. And she defies life to hit back. Here perhaps lies the full expression of her daring as a new woman. Through it she achieves complete visibility as a modern woman—the *Nabina*.

## Notes

1. Thomas Babington Macaulay, *Speeches, with the Minute on Indian Education* (London: Oxford University Press, 1935), 345.

2. Roy Armes, *Third World Film Making and the West* (Berkeley: University of California Press, 1987), 231.

3. Robin Wood, *The Apu Trilogy* (New York: Praeger, 1971), 13.

4. Andrew Robinson, *Satyajit Ray: The Inner Eye* (Berkeley: University of California Press, 1989), 160.

5. Marie Seton, *Portrait of a Director: Satyajit Ray* (London: Dennis Dobson, 1971), 181.

6. Chidananda Das Gupta, "Ray and Tagore." *Sight and Sound* 36, no. 1 (1966–67): 32.

7. Philip Kemp, "Satyajit Ray," in *World Film Directors*, Vol. II, ed. John Wakeman (New York: H. W. Wilson, 1988), 846.

8. Penelope Houston, "Ray's Charulata." *Sight and Sound* 35, no. 1 (1965–66): 31.

9. John Russell Taylor, "Satyajit Ray," in *Cinema: A Critical Dictionary*, Vol. II, ed. Richard Roud (London: Secker and Warburg, 1980), 824.

10. David Wilson, "*Charulata*," in *Magill's Survey of Cinema: Foreign Language Films*, Vol. II (Englewood Cliffs, NJ: Salem Hill Press, 1985), 518.

11. Ben Nyce, *Satyajit Ray: A Study of His Films* (New York: Praeger, 1988), 95.

12. Chidananda Das Gupta, *The Cinema of Satyajit Ray* (New Delhi: National Book Trust, 1994), 38.

13. Houston, "Ray's *Charulata*," 31.

14. Wilson, "*Charulata*," 519.

15. Houston, "Ray's *Charulata*," 32.

16. Wilson, "*Charulata*," 519.

17. Ibid., 519.

18. Nyce, *Satyajit Ray*, 93.

19. Kemp, "Satyajit Ray," 846.

# four

# Aranyer Din Ratri: Rewriting Self and Nation

**R**ay made Aranyer Din Ratri/ *Days and Nights in the Forest* in 1970 when he was coming increasingly under attack for being out of touch with the urgent problems of post–Independence India. He was also making Marxist critics very unhappy by refusing to name a political ideology in which he believed. Although he never did oblige them, there was a noticeable shift in the setting and subject matter of his films, starting with *Aranyer Din Ratri*. The film inaugurates a self-conscious "political" phase as Ray sets out to grapple with an India now almost an alien country in terms of its political and moral climate. With Nehru's death six years previously, the dream of a new progressive nation had floundered. India had become another Third World country saddled with debts, unemployment, inflation, and corruption. As Ray's generation, raised on the idealism of the '50s, felt hopelessly betrayed, it was left to the artists who had shaped their dreams to try and define what had gone wrong. While *Aranyer Din Ratri* would set the ground for Ray, his subsequent films—especially the Calcutta trilogy—would take up the challenge.

According to Das Gupta, in these post–*Charulata* films, Ray embarks on a "search for identity" with the new post–Independence generation that "does not share with him the full value of the Indian Renaissance."[1] Brought up to respect survival skills in the urban jungle, this new bourgeoisie has no sense of empathy with the values of a bygone era. They want to get ahead in the rat race, even if it means sacrificing their morals. For Ray, such pragmatism holds little appeal, especially since it makes people callous and insensitive. But despite his sense of alienation, he seeks to understand them—especially how they are redefining the India in which he lives. This reinvention of a nation becomes the very crux of the film, and it provides Ray with an opportunity to cover issues that are relatively new to his cinema such as class, racism, power, money, and consumerism. *Aranyer Din Ratri* thus functions on several levels, dealing with the debasement of the middle-class male, the corruption of urban culture, the enduring legacy of neocolonialism, and, above all, the formation of a new false hybridity—all of which point to a serious crisis in modernity. Moreover, Ray's choice of four flawed, confused, and unhappy antiheroes suggests a significant scaling down of the human subject.

In the film, based on Sunil Ganguly's novel of the same name, four friends—all Bengali males—leave Calcutta to spend a few days in the forests of Palamau. Despite their differences in education and upbringing, they belong to the moderately well-off, upwardly mobile middle class. Ashim is a young executive who is doing well at his job; Sanjoy is Labour Officer in a jute mill; Hari is a sportsman who has recently been jilted; Sekhar is unemployed. All four display their city-bred neurosis from the start, especially their insecurity about jobs, success, money, and women. Not having bothered to book rooms in advance, Ashim bribes the *chowkidar* (the caretaker of a government resthouse) into letting them stay there. They spend their first night drinking at the local liquor shop, during which Hari is attracted to Duli, a Santal tribal woman. Next morning, by sheer chance, they meet the Tripathi family from Calcutta at their country cottage. The family consists of father Sadasiv, daughter Aparna, widowed daughter-in-law Jaya, and her eight-year-old son Tublu.

The rest of the film is built around a series of encounters in which the men's pretensions are gradually undermined. As this "comedy of embarrassments"[2] develops, Ray pairs off Ashim with Aparna, Sanjoy with Jaya, Hari with Duli. Only Sekhar is left alone. When Jaya makes a physical overture to the inhibited Sanjoy, he flounders. Hari makes love to Duli in the forest and, on the way back, is beaten and robbed by Lokha, the servant, whom he had earlier accused of theft. Only Ashim and Aparna seem close to some kind of understanding. When the Tripathis abruptly leave, the men have nothing left to do but return to Calcutta.

## Very Impotent Persons: The Bhadralok of the '70s

Ray could have set his film in the city itself, but by taking the men out of their familiar world he is able to better expose their inadequacies. There is a sense that these *are* displaced men, without a stable identity or conception of their place in history and society. As Soumitra Chatterjee, who played Ashim, remarks, "[they] live in nothingness . . . they are nowhere people."[3] By setting them apart from one another, Ray wants us to see them both as distinct individuals as well as social types who constitute the new *bhadralok* of the '70s. And he comes up with a sexual metaphor to define their dysfunctionality.

Just before Ashim bribes the *chowkidar* into letting them stay in the resthouse, Sekhar introduces himself and his friends to the uncomprehending caretaker as "VIPs." He then proceeds to describe each one in superlative terms, until Ashim tells him to shut up and

buys off the man with a five-rupee note. Later in the film, lit up by
the headlamps of the car in which the women are traveling, a dead-
drunk Ashim will loudly proclaim in English that they are "very
important persons," which comes out sounding like "very impotent
persons." No self-definition could be more appropriate for a group
given to much rhetoric and posturing, but who can rarely match
words with deeds. Their forebears, the males of *Charulata*, may have
displayed little practical wisdom but they were men of learning and
noble ideals who spearheaded reform and progress. Ray shows how
their descendants are deficient in every respect—an emasculated
generation, entirely unworthy to lead India.

Of the four, Ashim, who acts as boss, is the worst behaved. Full
of his own sense of superiority, he is chauvinistic with women and
condescending toward those he considers socially inferior. As the
successful company executive, he is materially the best well-off. The
proud owner of a car, he is eager to invest in a house and settle down
to middle-class respectability. He likes the empowering feel of
money and has no scruples about bending his morals to make the
most of a situation. As we become privy to Ashim's memory of a
cocktail party, we sense that he is a good player with the appropriate social graces that win favor at the top. According to Pauline Kael,
"Ashim is much more like what Apu might have turned into if he
had been corrupted."[4]

However, what saves him from total crassness is an underlying
sensitivity and self-consciousness. He can rationalize his impulses and
his shortcomings—especially "the compromises he's been willing to
make to be successful."[5] When Sanjoy points to the ascending curve
of his career, he glumly admits: "The more I'll rise, the more I'll fall."
There is a deep sense of failure—something that will haunt all of
Ray's protagonists in the Calcutta trilogy. Coupled with this feeling
is a regret for a lost innocence. When he and Sanjoy once slaved away
at a literary journal, they clung tenaciously to the high standards they
set. Now Ashim feels all the effort he puts into his work is directed
toward loss. It is such introspection that will propel him toward a ten-

tative self-knowledge at the end. While Ray makes him arrogant and ill-mannered, he also reserves his larger sympathies for him.

If Ashim represents the drive, confidence, and egocentricity of his class, Sanjoy personifies many of its inhibitions and insecurities. Ray presents him as an example of the educated bourgeois Marxist whose political pretensions are proved to be sham at every turn. Although he displays a concern for the underdog, when the time comes for action he is "so overwhelmed by self-doubt"[6] that he fails hopelessly. This failure to act will become a major issue in *Pratidwandi/The Adversary* (1970), where Ray will treat it as a specific middle-class malady. During their drunken orgy on the first night, Ashim neatly sums up Sanjoy's bourgeois conformism with "[y]ou'll slave at a job, defer to your boss, live with your wife, and you'll be a complete Bengali middle-class conventional good boy."

One of the sources of Sanjoy's diffidence, Ray suggests, is the larger economic and social context of the middle-class home. Unhappy like Ashim with his professional life, Sanjoy claims he has a thousand reasons to give up his job, but cannot because his family—his parents and younger brother—depend on his wages for survival. Within the middle-class joint family, the individual cannot be motivated by self-interest alone. Sanjoy has to consider his obligations as son and elder brother before he can carve out his own space. Thus his vulnerability has deeper roots than may be apparent at first.

In such company, Hari seems a complete misfit, a man "of impulse, of action rather than reflection."[7] What he lacks by way of education or social courtesies he makes up with brawn. He defines his self-worth solely by his physical prowess—how good he is with his cricket bat. But muscle-power alone, he discovers, cannot buy him love, at least not in the city. Rejected by a sultry social sophisticate for his inability to write a proper reply to her five-page letter, Hari retaliates with brute force by grabbing her hair. Her slap shames his virility. Nursing his bruised ego in the forest, he lets out his deep insecurities through sex and acts of pure belligerence. For Ray, such displays of coarse behavior point to the repression, anxiety, and simmering violence that underlie the civilized veneer of this class.

Ray adds to this trio the jobless Sekhar whose carefree, moronic nature acts as a foil to the self-importance displayed by the others. Nyce describes him as a comic figure who refuses to be dislodged from his persona into "deeper and more troubling areas of experience."[8] Indeed, he remains free from the neuroses of the men, never gets drunk nor lusts after women. It is this self-contentment that makes him the most complex of the four, because it is so hard to account for. He remains happy to the end while the men struggle to recover from their various humiliations.

## Going Into the Forest

After *Pather Panchali* and *Aparajito*, this is Ray's first foray into nature, but it does not generate a pastoral vision in which the corrupt city is pitted against a redemptive rural world. Traditionally, the forest in India was viewed as a retreat, associated with the study of the scriptures and, above all, with renunciation, self-searching, and, finally, the quest for union with God. It is where the aging householder went to live and meditate after giving up home and society. But in this film the regenerative forest turns out to be physically bare, shorn of its flora and fauna (the animals now perform in the circus). Its inhabitants, the Santals, are no better off, debased by money, drink, and urban sprawl.

Within the antipastoralism of *Aranyer Din Ratri* the forest becomes a symbol of a lost mythic past, a source-culture rich in spiritual potential that has been destroyed by indifference and materialism. If it once nurtured civilization, it has now become the casualty of its own creation. For the corruption of a culture to be complete the root must atrophy as well. Thus Ray links the death of this ancient-forest India with the collapse of the modern postcolonial state. The India that was promised at its forest-birth is now simply a mockery of that original.

For the men, the journey into the forest is linked from the start to a search for renewal. Shortly before the credits appear we see the car stop at a gas station. Ray cuts to a medium shot of a hand feeding a nozzle into the empty tank while in the background Sekhar chatters away about the forest he is dying to see. In a single frame Ray juxtaposes his metaphor of renewal with the mythic overtones inherent in the word "forest."

But, as we become acquainted with the four, we realize that even if the old spiritual forests existed, these flawed men would never attain salvation. There emerges a rich sense of irony as we watch them bring along precisely what the Hindu texts urge all forest dwellers to shun: Excessive desire for sexual and material gratification; a fixation with money and power; class and caste consciousness; and the dominance of ego. For Ray, these are the very evils that have eroded the foundations of public moral life in India. By bringing along such baggage, the four world-weary men turn this journey into a travesty.

The men's first impulse is to shed their urban inhibitions and "go wild," seeking in such abandonment a return to a primeval state of freedom. As Ashim later tells Aparna, given their job-centered, regimented lives, rules need to be broken as soon as they relinquish the city. They don't shave, they bathe out in the open, get gloriously drunk, dance in the road, and burn their only newspaper in a symbolic snapping of ties with civilization. But as it turns out, getting back to nature does not serve as an escape but "a reiteration of each character's obsessions, problems, and vices dislocated to a new setting."[9] Although the city appears only in two brief flashbacks (Hari recalls his jilting and Ashim his cocktail party), it dominates their lives and crops up continuously in their conversations and attitudes. Sekhar misses the races; Hari longs for news about the cricket test match; Ashim and Sanjoy complain about the rat race. Moreover, as soon as the women show up, the men revert to their urban selves and begin to shave and behave "appropriately." When the women catch them bathing, they squirm with embarrassment. Going wild calls for a certain sensibility that the men clearly lack. Their incipient acts of nonconformism, as the wise Aparna points out to Ashim, only render them childish. This paradox—of being in the city when they are in the forest—becomes central to the film.

Since letting go also implies libidinal release, the men's journey acquires a specific sexual context as the forest holds out for them the allure of uninhibited, liberating sex. As Sanjoy reads aloud from a travel book, he conjures up an eroticized landscape, all curves and hills, where the Santals live with their ever-youthful bare-breasted women. For such sexually repressed men it sounds too good to be true; a real Eden complete with near-naked women fully bears out their fantasies. As if to corroborate what they hear, Ray cuts to the forest flashing past the car window and adds a soundtrack featuring tribal melodies and a choir of women's voices. The forest is thus rendered lush, erotic, and female. But soon after, when he abruptly switches to fast motion from Sekhar's point of view (but really the men's collective point of view), the trees go out of focus. Suddenly the forest is seen through short-sighted eyes, "an alien landscape"[10] to those who have never had any real contact with it. It is Ray's first hint that this search for sexual liberation, like the attempt to shed the city, is doomed. Sure enough, the men soon discover that sex in the forest is warped by deep inner tensions. In fact, it figures prominently in two of their worst humiliations.

The first involves Jaya and Sanjoy. We have noticed how she has been flirting with him and how he finds such attention self-empowering. But his moment of truth comes when she invites him home. While he waits in the living room, she changes her widow's white *sari*, puts on jewelry and makeup, then, transformed into a resplendent and sensuous woman, offers herself to him. But the sexually timid Sanjoy loses out to the repressions of his class. Even when she takes his hand and presses it against her bosom, all he can do is pull back, leaving her with a terrible sense of rejection. Ray shows how it is always men who can neither help themselves nor the women who need their help. In contrast to the pathetic Sanjoy, Jaya comes across as a strong and forthright woman. She also lives within the constraints of her society but, unlike him, once she enters the open space of the forest, she makes a real bid for freedom.

It is in this same forest that Hari has sex with Duli, the Santal woman, and grievously suffers for it. For a man "who is all unmediated sexual drive,"[11] she constitutes the exotic, promiscuous sexual Other with whom he can engage in pure lust. Since urban women intimidate him (especially after the jilting), he feels safe with a "primitive" tribal who poses no intellectual threat. In fact, he seeks to empower his ego by having her submit sexually to him, thus erasing the memory of his rejection.

The sex scene—"more like a rape than seduction"[12]—begins with Hari dragging Duli by force into the forest. When they make love, he holds her down, relishing his ascendancy. But if there is any "liberation," it is short-lived. The whole sex-as-empowerment caper collapses when Hari, walking home, is knocked out cold by Lokha, the servant, whom he had earlier assaulted. It is the price Hari pays for his false, loveless sex. As he lies groaning on the forest floor, the myth of the virile, invincible body is shattered forever.

Thus the men fail on all fronts: They are denied spiritual and sexual liberation as well as a return to a primitive state of innocence. It remains to be seen what the outcome will be to their other and most significant journey—the journey to discover and rewrite India. Since Ray deals with this issue in a later work as well, it would be appropriate to focus first on that film.

## Rewriting a Nation

In a key scene in *Shatranj ki Khilari/The Chess Players* (1977), General Outram, the British Resident of Lucknow, asks his ADC, Captain Weston, to translate Oudh into English. The year is 1856, and Oudh is a province in north India that Outram is about to annex. Not knowing any Urdu, Outram cannot make sense of the culture nor of the king, Wajid Ali Shah, whose extravagant lifestyle completely baffles him. Since Wajid's court knows no English, the bilingual Weston is his only ally in this fact-finding mission. Outram's project is motivated not just by a white man's curiosity about the exotic Orient, but by the needs of *realpolitik*. He knows fully well that the annexation is illegal—the British are bound by a treaty to honor the sovereignty of the king. But under direct orders from the governor general, Outram has no choice but to do his job and somehow salve his conscience. Thus he sets out to *rewrite* Oudh in English, replacing its cultural signifiers with English ones, distorting its textual meanings in the process.

As Weston translates specific social and cultural practices into English, Outram judges them outside their contexts according to an English moral yardstick shaped by the prejudices of Victorian orthodoxy. For example, when Weston describes the king as having twenty-nine *muta* (temporary) wives or reading a poem on the loves of the *bulbul* (the Persian nightingale) at a *mushaira* (a gathering of poets)—acceptable sexual and literary practices of a king within that culture—Outram decides that this very un-English Wajid must be a *bad* king. He calls him "frivolous, effeminate, irresponsible, and worthless," thus finding the justification he needs to proceed with his job. The annexation of Oudh becomes, in effect, first an annexation by language, through a text jointly reconstituted in English by Outram and his ADC.

In Ray's films set after Independence, there is a fascinating reversal of this situation. The British are nowhere in sight yet their language lives on, spoken by India's ruling elite, the Westernized bourgeoisie. English has ceased to be a foreign language but, fully assimilated like those other British exports, the railway and telegraph, is now the constitutional language of India. For Ray, this reversal is crucial in defining the postcolonial ethos in contemporary India. In the problem-centered films about urban life it is the *form* of this reversal that becomes a major issue. In their glass-and-concrete office blocks, Ray shows how his Bengali executives are vigorously engaged, like Outram, in rewriting an entire culture in English, except that, as Ray is quick to underline the irony, they are rewriting *their* culture and *their* India in English.

In the Calcutta trilogy, Ray will focus frequently on the corporate world for this investigation of neocolonialism. His Western-educated, English-speaking elite, born around the time of Independence, have never seen white men on the streets of Calcutta and yet they model their attitudes, values, and thinking on them. In fact, they have not only inherited the reins of power, but all the traits of their former colonizer. They display the worst forms of class-consciousness, snobbery, and racism toward anybody they deem inferior in rank and status. As Kael remarks, they have "internalized the master race. . . . Their status identity is so British that they treat all non–Anglicized Indians as non-persons."[13]

Kael describes *Aranyer Din Ratri* as "perhaps the subtlest, most plangent study of the cultural tragedy of imperialism the screen has ever had."[14] By emphasizing the English the four men speak and the contexts in which they speak it, Ray examines the role language plays in the transmission of an imperialist ideology and in the construction of nation and self. He shows how this post–Independence generation is reinventing India by rewriting it in English, how by choosing English signifiers for things intrinsically Indian they are engaged in an elaborate myth-making process to ensure the creation and survival of their "India." Within the framework of a hierarchical structure where power is assigned to a group, such an immersion in the imaginary becomes a way of consolidating that power. Language is a means by which the imaginary is invested with reality, the image authenticated as truth, *a* version made *the only* version. "India," then, becomes an "English" text for an elite who inscribe their histories, their passions, and their dreams in it; and it becomes a conceptual space for the redefinition of self and identity. The "other" India, the historical India of cultural and linguistic diversity, of inequalities and injustices, of caste and class divisions, is simply ignored or rewritten to fit the official version.

Once outside their familiar city, the four men in *Aranyer Din Ratri* run into an India that they barely know, which does not quite fit their pseudo–Western version and that, therefore, must be rewritten into an acceptable form. When the elder Tripathi calls them "tourists," the label makes sense—they *are* tourists in their own country. The film develops through a series of encounters they have with people from different social and ethnic backgrounds who con-

stitute a microcosm of Indian society. In this respect the film comes
close to being a social and political allegory about India: What India
is and what those in power would like it to be.

Not only do the four meet men and women who are far more
Westernized and sophisticated than they are (the Tripathis and the
forest conservator), but also those who live on the fringes of society:
Palamau's poor, low-caste villagers and the Santals who have a long
history of oppression. While the men defer to the former, it is the
disenfranchised masses who pose the biggest challenge, since their
presence is a major threat to their vision of India as a single, unified,
powerful, bourgeois nation. Therefore the men rewrite them virtually out of existence by employing Western paradigms and analogies
that render them crude, ridiculous, and ultimately subhuman. They
judge them to be outside their culture, applying a set of criteria alien
to their social condition. Thus whenever English is spoken in their
presence or absence, it is in the contexts of race, class, and power—
to define exclusion.

But Ray's purpose in the film is not merely to show how texts
are rewritten and erased in this way, but also to critique the "writ-
ers" who rewrite their identities in the process. The more the men
talk in English before the locals, the more they seem to become like
their former colonizers, adopting their tone and manner as they
address the "natives." Underlying this neocolonial posturing is a
sense of fractured selves, of false values, of a lost integrity. The men's
rewriting of India in English embodies the selling of India by Indians
to the consumer-capitalist West. In fact, the men's deepest longings—sexual and materialist—are conveyed through this consum-
erist discourse just as they express their racism through an imperialist discourse. At such moments, Ray brings us face to face with the
destructive legacy of colonialism as it corrodes not only the moral
and spiritual values within a community, but teaches a generation to
dream of selfhood and nation in a foreign language.

## A Polyglot Language

Ray draws attention not only to the English the men speak but also to the new hybrid language they have inherited and reinvented. Throughout the film, English words and phrases crop up within spoken Bengali, just as English phrases are sprinkled liberally with Bengali words. The language of the colonizer, we discover, has generated a new form in postcolonial India.

Beginning with *Shatranj ki Khilari*, one can trace the evolution of English as an imperial language that nineteenth-century Bengalis in *Charulata* and *Devi/The Goddess* (1960) have mastered through Western education. Its mingling with Bengali is already evident during the Bengali Renaissance, but such a polyglot language is spoken only by upper-class males and usually in contexts linked to learning and high culture. While this is still apparent in a film like *Ghare Baire/The Home and the World* (1984), in *Kanchanjungha* (1962) we sense its transformation into a truly postcolonial language that embodies the pretensions and snobberies of the neocolonial elite. Its appropriation by the urban middle class comes to the fore in Ray's films of the late '60s and '70s, as this class uses it to describe their newfound sense of power and status.

Especially in *Aranyer Din Ratri*, we encounter a new idiom as this polyglot English becomes the discourse of urban malaise, of the rat race, of exhaustion and dissipation, and of the politics of survival. Through it the men endorse their new philosophy of pragmatism. They not only define their frustrations and failures but also use it to cheat, betray, and swindle. It is the English of the consumer-capitalist West, shorn of the vocabulary of nineteenth-century progressive idealism, grafted onto Bengali. In fact, it sounds more American than English.

Although one could argue that the contexts in which this language is spoken point to India's decadence as a nation, Ray is more concerned with establishing it as an *Indian* language. He shows how two diverse cultures have really assimilated, not one on top of the other, but by forging together a new identity that reflects the formation of a modern hybrid India. Since such a linguistic phenomenon is historically and culturally inevitable within a colonial and a postcolonial society, it is inseparable from the contemporary Indian ethos. To deny it is to be culturally inauthentic. At the same time, Ray wants us to note the irony that he will develop in *Aranyer Din Ratri* as the men who endorse hybridity through language will seek to erase it politically through their rewriting of nation and self.

## An "English" Forest

As the film starts with the four men on the road in Ashim's car, Ray puts out warning signs in case we get lulled by what seems to be a back-to-nature fable. The lush foliage soon gives way to bare trees and dry riverbeds. When the gas station suddenly crops up in the middle of this wilderness, displaying its big Caltex sign in English, we are not surprised. All Third World landscapes bear the marks of their exploitation, whether economic or imperial, and even so remote a place is not exempt. The resthouse, where the men make their final stop, also has a sign in English to designate the monopoly of a class: Only those with permission may stay there. We are not surprised to discover that the place is a leftover from the Raj, when British officials stayed there during their tours of duty.

For Ray, it is such writing in English that proclaims most insidiously to the illiterate Santals the fact of their otherness. Alien texts of a master race, they carve out an exclusive territorial space and displace an entire race by simply ignoring it. When Ashim reads the text out loud, the sound of his English confirms our feeling that this "English" forest does not belong anymore to its real inhabitants.

In the precredit sequence Sanjoy reads aloud from a Bengali travel book written about a hundred years ago by Sanjib Chatterji, who once lived in Palamau and had close contacts with the tribals. For Chatterji, Palamau is a real place inhabited by real people and he writes about the Santals without condescension, refusing to judge or exoticize them. As we listen to Sanjoy, we immediately sense the disparity between Chatterji's classical Bengali and the men's contemporary speech patterns, which are full of slang and English words. His decorous prose has a different sound that suggests not only a way of conceiving language, but a different value system altogether. He refrains from using a single English word whereas the men immediately start translating his text into English. His Palamau is recast through a Western analogy into a culturally inauthentic place, its bastardized identity like that of the men.

On hearing that the tribal women drink with their men and often beat them at it, Sekhar exclaims "Western society!" When Chatterji claims that the women are all young, Sekhar cuts in with "eternal youth." Not content to treat the forest or tribals for what they are, he must graft a set of foreign signifiers that are hopelessly incongruous. The real forest, with its problems of deforestation and the oppression of the tribals, is ignored. Instead, Sekhar's English words conjure a forest of desire and fantasy, one that ideally contains a Western society.

Since, in his Bengali middle-class milieu the sexes do not mingle freely and drink together (such socializing is usually restricted to the Westernized elite) nor do they flaunt their youth and sexuality, Sekhar associates such behavior with Western permissiveness. A woman drinking is bad enough, but unpardonable if she drinks with men and holds her own, since she threatens their hegemony as males. True to the hypocrisies and sham righteousness of his class, Sekhar prefers to see women stay on the lower rungs of the male hierarchy. That "primitive" tribals could engage in such audacious modernity is thus cause for scorn, and he delivers such scorn, appropriately, in English. By being ironic Sekhar not only puts down the cultural practices of the Santals, but by framing his ridicule through a Western analogy he displays the terrible snobberies of the urban elite—that too, partly through English.

Of the four, it is Sekhar (Kael calls him "a joke the British left behind"[15]) who uses English the most and has a habit of naming objects, events, and people in that language. Dusk in the forest is labeled "sunset," the resthouse is "locked," the market has a "tea stall," the forest is "romantic"—as if reality can be apprehended only in terms other than its own cultural signifiers. When the men decide not to shave, he pronounces them "all hippies." It is at his urging that Hari whoops like Tarzan and compares the sunset to one he saw in a Burt Lancaster movie. And it is Sekhar who sets fire to the English newspaper and claims to be rid of civilization. But as the camera zooms to the burning newspaper, we realize that there is no getting away from this "English" civilization. It will keep popping up, phoenix-like, from the ashes.

### Tribal Welfare

The tribals in India, who have existed since pre–Aryan times, have been subject to systematic exploitation and abuse as a minority. Deforestation, the illegal seizure of lands, urban sprawl, and migrations to the city have rendered their existence precarious. Most cinematic representations in India make no allusions to these issues, but tend to exoticize them as the Other. Ray, on the other hand, focuses on their survival as a marginalized people who cannot find fulfillment anymore within their self-contained world of ritual, sex, drink, and dance. When he shows the women dancing, we never see them whole but reduced to a montage of body parts. The dream of a community is thus broached and undermined at the same time. But Ray cannot refrain entirely from invoking the romantic stereotype when he casts Simi Garewal, a glamorous Bombay star, instead of a local Santal woman to play Duli. Only after hours of rubbing black dye into her fair skin could Simi metamorphose into a woman of the forest—a neat irony in itself.

After Sekhar meets Duli for the first time, he describes her to Hari as "Miss India," thus displaying again his myth-making tendency in English. There is a tremendous irony in turning a Santal woman into the national symbol of a country whose tribals have been consistently robbed and cheated. And yet as a living symbol of ancient India, who could be more deserving of the title? But Sekhar's Miss India is a bad joke that recalls Western consumer imports such as fashion shows and Miss India beauty pageants where women are commodities displayed on ramps. Nothing could be further from the impoverished world of the Santals, and nothing could degrade them more than this grotesque racist parody. Besides, "Miss India" is uttered in a wholly sexual context. Sekhar, spotting Duli drinking with other tribal women at the liquor store, induces Hari to fix his lustful gaze on her. There is a symbolic display of the "virgin" in public prior to her ravishment by the depraved male from the city.

Later, when Sekhar spots Aparna and Jaya for the first time, he proclaims them to be "not Santals," thus invoking racial segregation. The distinction he makes in English boils down to this: Since the two women from the city are upper-caste "respectable" members of polite society, they are to be treated with decorum, but not the Santals who are "primitive" and therefore subhuman. The distinction is crucial, since all four men know that their identity depends on it. Thus for the men, Duli and her companions become the Other and social relations are defined in terms of sex or labor, both assuming exploitative forms and payoffs in money.

There are two more encounters with the Santals that provide further evidence of such "English" racism. At one point in the film Sekhar hires Duli and two other tribal women to perform menial jobs for the men at the resthouse. As he gives them money, he claims it is for "tribal welfare." This time Sekhar's English phrase is a mocking allusion to the schemes set up by the government of India to improve the lot of the tribals. Given the conditions in which the Santals live, we wonder what such schemes have really accomplished. Ironically, the only display of welfare in the film is by the tribals who cater to the men in lieu of a few rupees. As we see a once-proud people function as servants and cleaners, we sense their larger exploitation by those who clamor most for their improvement.

While the men lounge around and talk in a mixture of Bengali and English about transistors shaped like Vat 69 bottles and television sets in wristwatches, one of the women cools them with an old-fashioned rope-drawn fan. Ray juxtaposes the conversation with shots of the three women at work, but he especially singles out the woman with the fan who sits cross-legged on the floor, on the margins of the space occupied by the men, a symbol of the obedient servant-as-outsider. Clearly, the Empire is still going strong in India. Thus Ray not only establishes the political and cultural dimensions of this new capitalist-consumer power base, but includes within the same frame the uncomprehending victims of the new bourgeoisie—all significantly women. As the men empower themselves with their masculine talk about progress, the Santals, who don't understand a word, go on being the silent drudge of the nation.

Finally, drunk one night, the men jerk their hips on a country road and do the "Santal Twist" (as Ashim calls it). Later in the film when we see the Santals dancing, their rhythmic to-and-fro movement serves as an obvious contrast to the crude pelvic thrusts of the men. But perhaps much more offensive is the name Ashim gives to their dance. "Santal Twist" is a cultural abomination, two words crudely juxtaposed to produce a racial slur. Like the other visual and verbal East–West incongruities in the film, this one only serves to debase two different cultures. But the Santals come off worse because they are vulnerable. Their fragile culture on the verge of extinction cries out for intervention and action, not the trendy and exotic commercialization Ashim proposes. Like "Miss India," "Santal Twist" is a hideous parody of what is true and integral to a culture. Through such repeated distortions and dismissals the men make one fact very clear: The Santals have no place within their "English" nation.

## "Thank God for Corruption!"

The racism directed at the Santals resurfaces in the men's attitudes toward the locals, who are deemed inferior in terms of class and caste. Throughout the film Ray plays with terms such as *bhadralok* (gentlemen), *chotolok* (rude folk), *shabhya* (civilized), and *ashabhya* (uncivilized) within an inverted scale of values. The four men, who flaunt their superiority before such "backward" classes, turn out to be the real primitives, lacking in even basic human courtesies. But if

Ray wishes to invoke the notion of the noble savage, the tribals, as a lost, displaced people, cannot live up to such an ideal. Neither are the impoverished locals able to provide a definition of what being truly civilized is all about.

In the absence of a defining paradigm, class lines are rigidly imposed. Early in the film, when the men ask Lokha to accompany them to the resthouse, Sekhar, sitting in the front of the car with Ashim, refuses to yield space to the low-caste villager. Lokha has to sit in the back. With true bourgeois hypocrisy, Sekhar tells him how three people in front would make it difficult for the driver to maneuver the wheel. Later, Sekhar will shoo away a couple of locals who watch him bathe at a roadside well, gesturing at them as if they were dogs.

The only instance of a classless society is in the drinking scenes. The liquor shop serves as a watering hole where all gather—a fact that disconcerts Sekhar. He is the first to describe the people around him as *chotolok*, and immediately worries about his safety. Such a setup affects Ashim as well, for he is quick to draw a line of separation at the first hint of a challenge to his authority. When Lokha, who is now officially in their pay as servant, wants a share of his drink, he resists at once. By asking him to return the money left over from shopping, he reminds him of his place. Lokha is a domestic hired to work, not drink with his master.

Such disdain acquires a perverse form when it is directed at another low-caste local—the *chowkidar*, who by letting them stay at the resthouse without authorization has risked his job. He tells them repeatedly that his wife is gravely ill, that he has no time to cook or attend to the men, and yet they continue to make demands on him. It is only after Aparna makes Ashim see the appalling poverty and sickness inside the *chowkidar*'s room that "he's forced to confront his irresponsibility and class snobbery."[16]

What is so disturbing about such displays of racism and class consciousness is that they often occur when the men switch from Bengali to English. Ray makes this an issue when he shows how

English has become a language of subterfuge in which the men dress their snobberies so that they can display them before those for whom they are intended. (The British would have done the same with their "natives.") It is not only the tribals who have to suffer this atrocity, but all non–English-speaking minorities who live on the lower rungs of the class and caste system.

In the scene where Lokha's help is solicited to locate the rest-house, Sanjoy tells Ashim in English, "Ask him if he will come with us," which Ashim translates into Bengali, adding to it the lure of money. Sanjoy could very well have spoken to Lokha himself in Bengali, but by using English within his hearing he is quick to estab-lish a hierarchy based on exclusion. The men play at being British, Ashim becoming interpreter to Sanjoy. Suddenly, the familiar Indian setting is turned into a class-ridden landscape. Lokha is subtly told that he is different from them because he doesn't know English, and this lack points to other deficiencies, the most important being his status in terms of caste and class. Thus the sudden switch to English carries a message to Lokha: He knows he is being discussed, but not *what* is being discussed. That is precisely Sanjoy's point—to make him feel like a alien, to represent Lokha to Lokha as an incompre-hensible noun in the language of the dominant class.

This point is brought out even more forcefully when he shows up at the resthouse on the next morning. Sanjoy informs Ashim in English: "That boy is here." Soon after, "that boy" becomes "*the boy*," hired to run errands and take care of their groceries. Sanjoy's choice of word immediately conjures up the ghost of imperialism, except that it is a very real ghost as Ray goes on to show how Lokha is treated with extreme suspicion and condescension by the men, eventually getting beaten up by Hari for a theft he never commit-ted. Thus Sanjoy's two allusions to Lokha in English bring about his devaluation from local man to low-caste illiterate to hired hand bought with money.

Money is the other context in which English is frequently spo-ken in the film, as it retains, even in the forest, its urban signifiers of

power, status, and greed. By far the most blatant example of enslave-
ment by money is in the way Hari "buys" Duli. At the liquor shop
during their first meeting, the drink-besotted Santal asks him for a
share of his drink. When she calls him *babu*—master—power relations are defined at once. Aroused, he asks her to dance for him. But
when she tells him that another man paid her five rupees for the
same service, Hari senses a threat. To outbid this rival he pulls out his
wallet and pays her twenty-five rupees. When Sekhar tries to stop
him a brawl nearly breaks out. Nobody has the right to touch his
money. For this deeply insecure, phalliocentric man, his wallet
defines his virility.

When Ray links money to English, it is inevitably to emphasize
power and corruption. The most vivid example of this is the bribe-
giving scene. As they stand tall in their Western clothes before the
cowering *chowkidar*, the men first physically assert their power over
him. Then Ashim offers him the money. As the crisp rupee notes
exchange hands, Sanjoy, who is off-screen, reacts with "Thank God
for corruption!" The English phrase subtly enforces the equation
Ashim makes between power and money. The *chowkidar*, with his
sick wife and hungry children, gets the message at once. As a result,
the moral issue gets pushed aside, a casualty of the politics of power
and hunger.

The allusion to corruption is, of course, deeply ironic and betrays
Sanjoy's guilt as well as his resignation about the crisis of values in
contemporary India. His English phrase conveys more succinctly
than any Bengali phrase could the tragedy of colonialism. Not only
is there a sense that the dirty work of imperialism has morally and
spiritually ravaged the country, but that it has corrupted the class
who now rules it. Thus Sanjoy creates a link between past and present, between the forging of a system of exploitation and its consoli-
dation in a different era. But despite his "confession," he is so overcome by cynicism that he finds it impossible to act. Thus as a passive
witness to the bribe, he becomes an accomplice, a victim of history,
crippled by a legacy that will not let him protest a moral outrage.

## Correct English Phrases

Because Ray quickly loses patience with such people, he spends most of the second half of *Aranyer Din Ratri* unmasking their pretensions and hypocrisies. The men maintain with the local illiterates a certain facade that begins to crack as soon as they meet people from the city who speak not only in English, but in *better* English than they do. The bourgeoisie has its own caste system, and in the company of the better-educated, cosmopolitan upper middle class, the men feel terribly insecure. Suddenly, their much-vaunted English dries up or sounds utterly fake and contrived, nothing more than a bunch of clichéd phrases behind which they hide their pettiness. For Ray, such a betrayal of self is inevitable given its falseness, and, in turn, it betrays the falseness of their project—to rewrite India in English.

The men meet their match when the forest conservator arrives and orders them out of the resthouse for having occupied it illegally. For the first time there is a dramatic reversal as the men speak in Bengali and cringe before an authority figure who speaks English with an ease and confidence they clearly lack. It is Ashim, supremely confident in his rhetorical skills and his ability to browbeat his opponents, who takes on the challenge of persuading the conservator to let them stay. Ray uses the scene not merely to focus on Ashim's subsequent humiliation, but to introduce one last English-speaking authority figure.

Of all the neocolonials Ray has portrayed so far, the conservator is the most suave, the most urbane. When he argues with the men in his clipped British accent he becomes a living symbol of the legacy of the Raj. Ashim does not reach for his wallet this time, nor does Sanjoy try to hide his disdain behind his English. Proven inferior on all fronts—class, status, power, and language—and found guilty of trespassing, they have to endure their humiliation—in English. Visually the scene is meant to recall the earlier group scenes between the men and locals. With exquisite irony Ray shows how the men, stripped down and vulnerable, begin to sound and look like their victims. But he also inserts the scene to reaffirm a crucial fact, that the hierarchy of power *within* this neocolonial bureaucracy is determined to a large extent not only by who speaks English but, above all, *how* he or she speaks it. He returns to this issue at several points in the film.

Before they meet the conservator, the men have to deal with the ranger, his subordinate in rank and class, who dutifully recites the *dos* and *don'ts* to them but does not have the personality to enforce them. The men treat him with derision, as a petty provincial officer without good breeding or refinement. When he displays a painful stammer it is bad enough, but when he stutters out a bizarre English full of archaic Britishisms and Bengali words, they show him no mercy.

There is something very pathetic about the ranger's attempts to assert his authority by speaking a language he improperly knows. The stammer metaphorically represents his identity crisis, how bad he is at this pretense. But above all it shows how foreign English is to a man whose education has been in Bengali and who belongs to a different class from that of the men. The ranger persists because he identifies his fragile sense of power with the handful of English words and phrases he has crammed into his head.

Before the conservator arrives, Ray includes a scene at the resthouse in which the ranger is shown barking orders at the *chowkidar*, who scampers around like a dog trying to set things up for the conservator's stay. The ranger is no longer the meek provincial, feeling inferior in the presence of an urban class; when it comes to playing boss to his subordinates such as the cowering non–English-speaking *chowkidar* (his "inferior" on all fronts) he relishes the role. But when the conservator addresses him, the ranger is all deference. The same fractured English continues but the tone has changed to one of obsequiousness. Thus Ray defines a relationship between spoken English and the enunciation of power in which superior accents and correct syntax help to determine who stays at the top, and who below.

We see this again in a different context when the women drive up to the resthouse to return Hari's wallet, which he had dropped while playing badminton with them. They surprise Ashim, Sanjoy, and Sekhar, who are bathing in their shorts at a roadside well. The men are so overcome by their bourgeois sense of propriety that Sanjoy dives for cover, while Ashim and Sekhar stand red-faced with embarrassment. It falls upon Sekhar, covered with soap and looking utterly ridiculous, to conduct civilities, which he does by rattling off some stock English phrases—"So kind of you!," "Have a nice trip!," "Thank You"—in a thick Bengali accent. Later, he tells the men how thrilled he was rattling off "correct English" phrases in front of those upper-class sophisticates from the city. But the women, who can see through his pretensions, pay him no attention, reply in Bengali and depart, leaving him more vulnerable than before.

Insecure like the ranger in "superior" company, Sekhar tries to hide his real and metaphorical nakedness behind these inanities in English. As at other moments in the film, he could have easily switched to Bengali instead; but trying to live up to an impossible ideal of class, he fails miserably. His stock English phrases are also meant to remind us of the frequent "thank yous" and "sorrys" that the characters utter in this film. Since both forms are absent in Bengali, people have to resort to English to prove that they are sufficiently civilized. Thus, in its juxtaposition of Eastern prudery and exaggerated British civility, the scene encapsulates the entire history of cultural displacement.

## The Memory Game

Ray's final disillusionment with this generation is felt most keenly in the memory game during which the men and women sit on picnic blankets and engage in a bout of name-dropping. The game requires each player to recall in sequence the names of famous people that the others have invoked, before adding a new name. As the game proceeds, the internationally renowned—Marx, Mao, Cleopatra, Shakespeare—mingle with those nearer to home such as Tagore, Rani Rashmoni, and Mumtaz Mahal. But first, the three key figures of the Indian freedom movement—Gandhi, Nehru, Azad—are named by Sekhar. There is a neat irony in this, since their vision of a secular, unified India will be rendered a sham by the game's bizarre juxtapositions and lack of coherence. Instead of a country with a cohesive identity formed by diverse strands, India, we discover, is a nation of fragments, a collage that does not yield shape or meaning. To recall the famous in this context seems a farce. The game serves more as a roll call of history and culture by the middle class who yearn for a place in it. Through their recital, they wish to experience some pride as citizens of a spurious nation. As they name their heroes, we wonder whether the legacy of the founding fathers has any substance whatsoever in their lives.

Ray has made repeated allusions in the film to names (Aparna is also known as Rini, Tublu as Anandamukul) and memory (while Jaya is forgetful, Aparna has a phenomenal memory—she can even remember events that occurred when she was two years old). For Ray, the amnesia that most people display during the game is a sign of their inability to focus, learn, and retain. The lessons of the past are quickly lost on them. If one is to acquire a sense of self in relation to history and engage with a dynamic future, then it is absolutely vital to remember, to connect time past with time present. Only Aparna seems qualified to forge such an identity and embrace such a future.

In an earlier scene, Ashim, while going through her books and record albums, had noticed a bizarre mix of titles: the Beatles, Vilayat Khan, Mozart, Bertrand Russell, Agatha Christie, the Metaphysical Poets. "I can't quite make you out" was his puzzled response. What he couldn't see was Aparna's extraordinary ability to encompass a diverse range of influences within her self. Thus she becomes a living symbol of the original dream of hybridity in which each unit would retain its separateness while constituting a complex, interrelated whole.

Ray denies us an India that has achieved such unity in diversity, but instead points to a false, pastiche nation. Rewritten over and over again to conform to the fantasies of the Westernized few, India is not a single, integrated nation of many creeds and cultures, but one of mismatched names and unresolved dreams. The unethical campaign to write off social and ethnic minorities, to establish an "English" India, and to reject an extraordinarily diverse social and political reality has broken its back. According to Scott Byron, the country has become a dumping ground for the world's culture. As he puts it, "[o]ne culture imposed on another has resulted in a humpty-dumpty fragmentation."[17] India can never be whole again.

Perhaps the scene that announces the death of the India of the founding fathers is the one in which the men engage in an act of sacrilege. Walking back from the liquor shop, dead drunk, they loudly sing "*Sara Jahan Se Accha Hindusthan Hamara*"/"More Dear Than My Heart Is My India." Composed by the nationalist poet Iqbal, this deeply patriotic song celebrates the oneness that underlies all diversity. The India that the men extol in their slurred voices is a gross parody of that dream.

## Notes

1. Chidananda Das Gupta, *The Cinema of Satyajit Ray* (New Delhi: National Book Trust, 1994), 89.

2. Tom Milne, "*Days and Nights in the Forest.*" *Sight and Sound* 41, no. 1 (1971–72): 49.

3. Andrew Robinson, *Satyajit Ray: The Inner Eye* (Berkeley: University of California Press, 1989), 194.

4. Pauline Kael, "*Days and Nights in the Forest,*" in Kael, *Reeling* (Boston: Little Brown, 1976), 141.

5. Ben Nyce, *Satyajit Ray: A Study of His Films* (New York: Praeger, 1988), 124.

6. Milne, "*Days and Nights in the Forest,*" 49

7. Ibid., 49.

8. Nyce, *Satyajit Ray*, 121.

9. Gaylyn Studlar, "*Days and Nights in the Forest,*" in *Magill's Survey of Cinema: Foreign Language Films*, Vol. II (Englewood Cliffs, NJ: Salem Press, 1985), 751.

10. Milne, "*Days and Nights in the Forest,*" 48.

11. Nyce, *Satyajit Ray*, 121.

12. Kael, "*Days and Nights in the Forest,*" 141.

13. Ibid., 141.

14. Ibid., 141.

15. Ibid., 141.

16. Studlar, "*Days and Nights in the Forest*," 750.

17. Scott Byron, "*Days and Nights in the Forest*." *Film Quarterly* 25, no. 3 (1972): 37.

*five*

# Pratidwandi:
# The Nature of Inaction

I f in *Aranyer Din Ratri* Ray had moved out of the city in order to come to grips with it, in *Pratidwandi/The Adversary*, based also on a novel by Sunil Ganguly, he would confront it head-on. If the city came across more as a state of mind in that film, here it acquires a tangible, physical presence. In fact, it dominates *Pratidwandi* and the two subsequent films, *Seemabaddha/Company Limited* (1971) and *Jana Aranya/The Middle Man* (1975). Ray seems to have "reached the city at last."[1] The Calcutta trilogy, that the film inaugurates, will chronicle the moral and spiritual collapse of this new urban India. For Nehru it was the city, more than anything else, that stood for

India's future and the growth of its modernity. The trilogy will show the betrayal of that dream and the death of a whole cultural ethos.

Ray's choice of Calcutta is not simply because it is his city, but, as we know, it was here that the modern was conceived and brought forth. He identifies deeply with its history of progress and reform, its tradition of scientific and rational thinking, and its extraordinary cultural accomplishments. Despite its squalor and chaos the city would never lose its hold on him. In fact, he once described Calcutta as the most intellectually stimulating place in Asia and that he couldn't think of living anywhere else.[2]

But in the late '60s and early '70s Calcutta was no longer the same city, just as India, in the throes of major political upheavals, was rapidly transforming itself. There was the Bangladesh war, the exodus of refugees into India, large-scale government repression, and the declaration of a nationwide Emergency. Suddenly, as *Aranyer Din Ratri* showed, Ray's cherished values of the Bengali Renaissance were under assault from a new generation brought up not on idealism, but corruption and bureaucratic bungling. When the Naxalites, a Maoist group, called for armed revolution, Calcutta turned into a city of daily rallies, bomb blasts, and killings. Statues of Ray's cultural heroes were defaced. For the first time in his life, he toyed with the idea of leaving the city.

The trilogy, made against this background, is an artist's anguished response to the debasement of a whole culture. In it he portrays a city without hope, where corruption is rampant, jobs are rigged, mothers pimp for their daughters, and the unemployed wander the streets. His middle-class protagonists—all young men—are the victims of a dehumanizing rat race, struggling to hold onto their inherited values in the face of betrayal and compromise. It is the moral dimension of their individual tragedies that becomes the ostensible subject of these films.

Siddhartha, the protagonist of *Pratidwandi*, is a young man of twenty-five who gives up his medical studies when his father dies and then tries to find a job. At home, his brother Tunu talks about revolution while his sister Sutapa is unfazed by allegations that she is having a relationship with her boss. For Siddhartha, returning home every night after walking the streets, is like entering an airless, claustrophobic cell. When his friend Adinath takes him to a prostitute, it only serves to disgust him. The only positive development in his life is his friendship with Keya, who alone can relate to his sensitive nature. The film ends with an interview during which Siddhartha explodes with anger at the sheer callousness displayed by the authorities. Forced to leave his city, he accepts a job as a medical representative in a small town. It is here that he hears a bird call he had once heard as a boy, which has haunted him ever since.

There have been jobless young men in Ray's cinema before, but in a problem-based film like *Pratidwandi*, unemployment constitutes a center to which all events hark back. The search for a job provides a context for Ray to not only engage with the politics of urban survival, but with issues that he emphasized in *Aranyer Din Ratri* such as identity and the crisis of the post–Independence male. Once again, he turns to a generation born around 1947, that has the most potential to bring about change but invariably loses out to frustration and despair. However, unlike the men in *Aranyer Din Ratri* who are older and relatively well-off, Siddhartha belongs to a middle class for whom economic survival takes precedence over all other issues.

Ray turns Siddhartha into a brooding, introspective man with a smoldering vitality that often breaks out in flashes of anger. If the four men of *Aranyer Din Ratri* embodied urban burnout, he takes on the city with all the vigor, confusion, and terrible vulnerability of youth. As Ray's first deeply troubled man, who lacks even the fake self-confidence of the *Aranyer Din Ratri* quartet, Siddhartha's vacillations and inner contradictions, which extend to all spheres of his life, are symptomatic of an entire class that has succumbed to misguided idealism. He becomes the prototype of the decentered man whom we first encountered in the earlier film.

Siddhartha's dilemma is how to formulate a mode of action that will prove meaningful in a society rendered absurd by its inequities. Since old-fashioned heroics have no place in this world, the individual has recourse only to gestures that don't necessarily change anything but that present him with a chance to affirm his potential. Thus Siddhartha provides Ray with an opportunity to engage in a complex meditation on the nature of action and its antithesis—inaction. In fact, Ray's preoccupation with modernity in the film centers around his crisis—to act or not to act.

Siddhartha's vacillations often reflect Ray's own doubts as he tries to get close to this new post–Independence breed. While there is sympathy for Siddhartha's sensitivity and potential, there is no sense here of a clearly thought-out agenda or resolution. Ray seems content to let the film grow out of his protagonist's hesitancies and gropings, and even allows his point of view to be consistently ruptured by his unstable subject. Thus we have a vacillating artist who creates a highly fluid text and remains as elusive as the man he seeks to pin down. Siddhartha's dislocations become Ray's own dislocations, even more so as Ray sheds his classicism and adopts a jagged, disruptive style that subverts the framework of the conventional narrative. *Pratidwandi* is full of jump cuts, freeze shots, ellipses, and hand-held camera work as Ray tries to see Siddhartha on Siddhartha's terms. He also turns increasingly to his protagonist's memories, dreams, and fantasies to find an entry into his unconscious. Such an emphasis on the irrational is new to his cinema; in fact, it is more complex than that. What occurs in the film is a reformulation of consciousness as something that is not stable or grounded in rationality and whose shifts can only be described through a new vocabulary.

## Margins and Centers

Like Apu, Siddhartha carries the marks of his multiple dislocations. From his mother's accent we discover their status as refugees from East Bengal—victims of the 1947 Partition. As one of history's displaced who crossed a border even as he was born, Siddhartha now lives on the other side, in the margins of the political and geographical Other. This breeds a precarious sense of belonging, as he cannot precisely define his new borders or decide whether the side he is on is truly the side he wants to be on. Moreover, living in a city whose cultural and social space is deeply plural, he opts for a middle space where he can indefinitely postpone choice and commitment.

At the same time, it seems only appropriate that Calcutta should become his city of adoption and serve as a backdrop to his search for roots. Ray doesn't let us forget that it is a colonial creation and a Third World city, embodying the displacements of history and identity. Home to highrises and slums, the city is a hallucinatory mix of Western-style progress and appalling poverty. Functioning within a culture of such extremes, we sense Siddhartha's cultural dislocations as a postcolonial. He speaks English and Bengali separately as well as in a mixed format; his habits, clothes, even his dream of emancipation invoke Western paradigms. And his continuing battle with the colonized Indian bureaucracy affirms the postcolonial's struggle with an enduring foreign legacy. Like those of his generation, Siddhartha finds himself questioning his status as a citizen of this new India. Which India and whose India?

As a sort of preface to this saga of disruption, the film opens at a moment of rupture in Siddhartha's personal life. His father's death displaces him into the streets of Calcutta and into joblessness. In fact, we encounter him for the first time in front of the funeral pyre, shot in negative from which his image changes to positive. We thus meet the film's protagonist against a background of death and disintegration (the film will likewise close with a reference to death)—a portent of things to come.

Siddhartha's journey in *Pratidwandi* involves a margin–center dialectic: From margin to middle to center to margin. Living on the fringes of a system that denies him access, he has two options: To dismantle the center or negotiate with it. At first, he chooses the latter. Joining the rat race, although he knows interviews are rigged, becomes a strategy of negotiation. Predictably, it breeds hopelessness and a terrifying apathy as he tries to live out a lie. Ray often shoots Siddhartha with his arms folded, hugging his body, in a posture of vulnerability, occupying the space where two walls intersect. The shot neatly encapsulates his dilemma. This middle space when translated into the film's narrative becomes a metaphorical threshold from which he needs to step forward. The inability to act decisively, Ray suggests, points to a larger paralysis of will—the cultural legacy of an entire generation that lives in limbo. Early in the film Ray gives us a visual equivalent of Siddhartha's suspension as he shoots him from a high angle walking across a zebra line at a busy intersection. When he stops in the middle, his confinement within a geometric grid formed by vertical and horizontal stripes becomes immediately apparent.

And yet Siddhartha's indecisiveness acquires a complex ambivalence in the film, recalling Charu's boredom in *Charulata*. Ray describes it in terms of a highly active internal process, a psychological and emotional engagement that turns it from a negative condition into a productive one. Siddhartha thinks, feels, and grows under his skin of apathy. As he vacillates, questions, falls prey to self-doubts, he generates a dynamic entirely his own. Instead of his confusions leaving him at a dead end, we see him eventually fashion a personal choice out of them. Thus, paradoxically, apathy is *necessary* for Siddhartha to turn him into an activist, into an adversary. Above all, such self-questioning makes him supremely human.

In the film, Siddhartha's hiatus between action and inaction is emphasized repeatedly in the situations in which he finds himself. He imagines shooting his sister's boss with a gun, but it remains only a fantasy. He joins a mob about to lynch the driver of a car that has run over a child, but the sight of a terrified schoolgirl on the back seat stops him—he sees his own vulnerable self in her. But perhaps the scene that best describes Siddhartha's struggle to act is during his visit with Adinath to the prostitute.

Before that happens, quite early in the film we get a sense of Siddhartha's repressed sexuality when the sight of a well-endowed woman crossing a street makes him flash back to a class he attended on the female breast. Accustomed to keeping his lid down on his libidinal urges within a bourgeois setup, the only way he can disarm lust and displace it is through such drab fantasies. But in case we think all middle-class men are sexually inhibited, Ray gives us Adinath, who has no qualms about visiting a prostitute. He is the surrogate big brother and tempter who seeks to initiate Siddhartha into sex.

Even as they enter the house, Siddhartha complains of feeling confused. Children playing on the landing shout "Ready, steady, go!," but Siddhartha cannot make himself go. He sits white-faced in his chair while the prostitute, who works during the day as a nurse, takes off her uniform and in her bra and petticoat asks him to light her cigarette. When he complies, his gaze averted, Ray switches to negative to underline another moment of dislocation in his life. The tentative contact has only served to push him away from her. When Adinath disappears into the bathroom to help her with her bra hook, he stalks out in apparent disgust.

For Adinath, Siddhartha's failure to act is simply a loss of nerve, an inability to translate desire into practice that points to his bourgeois male tragedy. As he tells the prostitute: "He's hungry inside all right but just won't show it on his face." But Ray also suggests that Siddhartha is morally outraged, since he finds the whole business utterly degrading. We will see later how other motives can be imputed once Siddhartha's relationship to his sister Sutapa becomes clear.

## Thinkers and Doers

Adinath divides people into two categories: Those who think and those who act. As for himself, he belongs to the latter—a doer, who is guided by a self-serving pragmatism and scoffs openly at any pretense at idealism. He can dispense with morals and his conscience as long as he can exploit a situation for material benefits (we see him pilfering from a Red Cross box with which he has been soliciting donations). Thinking, for him, is a waste of time, especially if the thinker cannot transform his thoughts into action. As he cautions

Siddhartha when they visit the prostitute: "You don't come here to think." He is there for only one purpose: To satisfy his lust.

Siddhartha's problem, according to Adinath, is that he is a thinker who forever contemplates what he will never do. As he puts it: "What you want to do is only in your imagination; when it comes to actually doing it, you won't be able to." When Siddhartha talks like his brother about cleaning up the mess with a machine gun, Adinath laughs mockingly as he tries to picture him holding a sten-gun and hurling grenades. For one who vacillates—the hallmark of Adinath's thinker—there can be no revolution.

The conversation raises an issue that clearly interests Ray. For action to be meaningful, especially in a corrupt and unjust society, should it be necessarily political in nature? If "doing" indeed trans-lates into political doing or daring, then Siddhartha's conversion from thinker-worrier to agent-doer must involve some form of activism that subverts the system. At the same time, Ray is not inter-ested in narrow formulations that assert "everything is political." He defines Siddhartha's apathy not simply as a political issue but also as a complex psychological and cultural condition. In other words, he places his indecisiveness within the larger framework of his individ-uality and considers the self to be the real source of any productive action. As he explains: "I still believe in the individual and in personal concepts rather than in a broad ideology that keeps changing all the time."[3] For him, the true doer acts with purpose and feeling, with conscience and guts, drawing on his life—not in the apathetic, self-serving, and irresponsible way Adinath's pragmatism functions.

We learn from Naresh, a party official, that Siddhartha was polit-ically active as a student but that now all he cares for is finding a job. It makes Naresh wonder whether he has lost faith in politics. In real-ity, Siddhartha finds the exigencies of daily living far too over-whelming. Besides, he seems no longer confident that change can be brought about by subscribing to a political cause. He claims that he is simply tired of empty rhetoric and beginning to choke on the advice people give him. Predictably, he resists being drawn into the party by Naresh but accepts, in the end, the job that he finds him as a medical representative.

Siddhartha's political apathy could be criticized as a very bourgeois turning away from the public sphere to the private, from the collective to the self. No longer able to see himself as part of a movement for social justice nor define his place within a historical paradigm, he puts his personal problems over those of the group. His disillusionment can partly be ascribed to the failure of the leftist coalition in West Bengal in the mid-to-late '60s, which revealed rampant factionalism and corruption. What motivation could one find within a party or in its mandate for change? Siddhartha is faced, then, with the only remaining option: To become a militant like his Naxalite brother Tunu, who believes that the only bit of doing that has any worth is "doing" revolution.

Tunu is openly critical of his elder brother's middle space, which for him is the bourgeois space of complacency and compliance. To occupy it is tantamount to opting out of the struggle for a better world. He complains that Siddhartha is stuck in a rut and obsessed with one thing—finding a job. He's just rotting away. What would happen to him after he found a job? Siddhartha is cynical enough to reply that he would simply be a cog in the bureaucratic machine and rot away just as much as he is doing now. Tunu finds such hypocrisy appalling. Why must Siddhartha hold on to the bourgeois dream of job and respectability when he knows it's all wrong? Instead of complying with the system, he should do battle with it. His crises, for Tunu, are now centered around bourgeois nonissues such as finding a bomb with which he can blow up his sister's boss. And his crisis of identity, he would argue, is bourgeois to the hilt.

Tunu shows him the book he had once given him on his birthday: The complete works of Ché Guevara. Siddhartha ruefully remembers how he had to sell three medical books to purchase it— the price he paid for buying idealism. The economics of survival have now become more urgent than debates about revolution. Ché, in retrospect, seems to be the fond dream of an adolescent, too remote to be real for the job-seeking man. Looking into the mirror, he fantasizes himself whiskered and bearded like Ché only to turn away, embarrassed at such pathetic self-indulgence. Moreover, even if he could literally become Ché, would it really produce the Marxist utopia? Siddhartha seems to display all the despair of the jaded, demoralized revolutionary, except that he has never been one—only aspired to be one. Having come to strongly distrust ideologies, utopias, quick-and-easy political solutions, he seeks instead to engage directly with the reality at hand. He wishes to negotiate with it as an individual rather than let an ideology mediate and interpret it for him. He could read Ché, he tells Tunu, when he didn't have to worry about finding a job.

But for Tunu, a college student, who reads all the right books but hasn't been out in the world yet, the notion of a one-track mind holds enormous appeal. As a Naxalite, his only goal is to dismantle the bourgeois state. With single-minded devotion he has "totally erased the past in order to devote himself to a present whose justification will be the creation of a new undefined future."[4] Thus he finds it impossible to conceive of any form of action other than in political terms. Ray is wary of such ideologues who become fixated with one definition of truth. Commenting on Tunu's close identification with his cause, he points out how he's "become part of a total attitude" that has erased his identity as an individual.[5] The party does his thinking for him—"he, as a person, becomes insignificant."[6]

Later, Siddhartha has a dream triggered by Tunu's talk about public executions. He sees the blade of a guillotine come crashing down on his neck. His head upside down, mouth open hideously, he screams. In a subsequent dream he will witness Tunu face a firing squad with a smile of defiance on his face. Both dreams confirm what Siddhartha knows deep down—that he is much too human (or cowardly as Tunu would say) to stare death in the face and die for a cause. Caught, then, between Adinath's self-serving pragmatism and Tunu's ideological compulsion to act—two extreme forms of doing—Siddhartha retreats into the middle.

## A Face In a Faceless City

In a film in which medical metaphors proliferate, Calcutta is a city of festering sores, its ravaged body almost beyond cure. But even sick, the place retains its fascination for its citizens. Like Ray, Siddhartha admits that "[t]here's something about the city" and Adinath concurs—he cannot see himself living outside of it for even a minute. Life is "rotten" here, he claims, but it is still life. For him, other cities are either dead or dying. Calcutta then is a putrid city, but a city with a certain fatal charisma. To live in such a place, Siddhartha finds out, one cannot simply stay inert. The city pushes him up against his apathy and demands that he *do* something about it.

Ray captures the city's nervous energy with handheld shots, rapid tracks, zooms, and jump cuts that approximate the disjointed gaze of the jobless man of the streets. As in *Jana Aranya*, here also the street serves as a central metaphor. Siddhartha's history of multiple displacements, his search for the right path, his attempts to reach the center from the margins are all echoed in his peripatetic daily life. There is even a scene where he stands on the curb and contemplates the lines and arrows painted on the street as if his fate depends on reading the signs correctly.

As we see him walk, we sense his preference for the city's open anarchic space in which his roving eyes can fasten on anything and everything. Store signs, street signs, magazine stalls, billboards—all come under his gaze as he walks through a consumer dreamscape selling the good life. Such forms of "writing" are complemented by the writing on the wall: A rich and diverse political rhetoric in the form of graffiti, slogans, and posters. Siddhartha reads both languages, which deepens his crisis of choice. While the billboards urge him to dream the bourgeois dream, he cannot ignore the subversive content of the other texts. There is a collective political consciousness—however much splintered by parties and ideologies—that seeks to draw him in. Caught between these two discourses, he tries to hold onto his middle space, but not for long. The city of protests will not let him rest.

This is brought out very vividly in the scene where Siddhartha and his girlfriend Keya stand on top of a highrise building enveloped in a maelstrom of noise from the largest political rally ever held in Calcutta. As they are buffeted by the city's collective voice of discontent we wonder whether such an outpouring of rage will change anything—or remain mere rhetoric.

Ray's slow-tracking camera follows them, lending a fragility to their bodies and movements. They seem terribly vulnerable high above ground, tightly framed within space, their voices all but drowned out by the noise from the loudspeakers. As we see their private space brutally invaded, we ask how love can survive in this city. To see them alone for the first time in the film is only to know that they are *not* alone. Even far up, the city is simply inescapable. Still, their togetherness generates a certain warmth, although they talk about going away from the city, each to a different place.

Siddhartha has brought Keya here not to be merely alone with her but to show her Calcutta. From their point of view, we see the city and its landmarks invaded by the rally's swarming crowds. So far, Ray has shown us the city only from ground level, but now the overhead shot provides Siddhartha (and us) with a glimpse of an all-pervasive reality of unrest. We sense a large, complex pattern within which the bomb blast and the mob lynching exist as individual elements. Siddhartha cannot afford to focus on single details anymore, but must place his problems within this larger whole.

The conversation between him and Keya underlines this macro–micro relationship. He talks about his interview; she, about her father marrying her aunt—a fact that deeply pains her. Suddenly these personal issues do not seem isolated and separate but linked to the mass protest going on below. Not finding a job nor having to accept a new mother seems no less important than the larger problems being debated below. In a troubled world all issues are connected and become significant.

As we sense the smoldering violence below, we realize that the bomb blast, the mob lynching, the rally, and Tunu's guerrilla war are outlets through which the city vents some steam. They serve as rents and fissures in an urban volcano whose explosion cannot be indefinitely postponed. If Siddhartha must act, as the city urges him to, then it must be as an individual asserting his uniqueness through his choice without sacrificing his public consciousness as citizen. But how does one forge such a gesture and maintain its independence within a mass-defined, protest? How to ensure that it does not become a calculated political gesture to appease some party boss? How does one retain what is intrinsically one's own and not lose it to the crowd?

As Siddhartha ponders over these questions, the dilemma threatens to boil down to an "I" versus "them" issue. We have noticed before how he seems reluctant to identify himself with the people who share his space. Compared to the disenfranchised—the pavement dwellers, the jobless, the dropouts—who surround him, Siddhartha is only marginally better off, but he doesn't quite see himself as one of "them." His awareness is signaled only by a few point-of-view shots of squatters huddled on the pavement; there is no sustained gaze at the deprivation around him. As one of history's displaced, living in a city of the dispossessed, Siddhartha cannot yet see himself in their ranks. But how long can he hold himself aloof? The rally scene, by placing him above ground, proves that even here he cannot shut out the city nor the call it sends out to him.

Ray suggests that Siddhartha's problem is compounded by his medical training, which has provided him with an inner vision or X-ray vision with which he dissects the world (as he once dissected bodies with a knife). His double vision enables him to see men and women in their social and personal contexts as well as simply being biological specimens. We have already seen how the woman crossing the street provoked a dissection. In a city such as Calcutta, where life after all is a quotidian affair, it doesn't take much effort to pare people down to the bone. The recurring shots of people walking, hanging out of buses, and assembling at the rally define the city as a place where men and women are reduced by their sheer numbers to a shapeless mass. Perhaps because he can "see" their terrifying sameness, Siddhartha wishes to pull himself away from the crowd.

That this is an issue that haunts him becomes evident in his conversation with Keya on their first outing. He tells her how people are the same inside, that each cadaver cut open reveals the same set of bones, tissues, veins, and arteries. But she resists and points out how even two people cannot be alike. While he attributes difference to education, temperament, and social circumstance, she defines difference in terms of looks: How a person's eyes can betray his or her goodness. But he is more wary and less trusting: Looking or seeming good, he cautions, doesn't ensure goodness of heart—one could easily be in error. "Better not be in error," is Keya's response, as the shot fades to black.

Her vision of people as individuals, rescued from the anonymity of mere bodies, serves to counter the ex-medical student's philosophy of the dissection table. She sees them as human beings who breathe, think, and feel, each unique in his or her way. And his not-so-veiled cynicism about goodness cannot kill her idealism: She persists in believing in it for its own sake. For Ray, such faith amounts to a redemptive vision of humanity in a city teeming with faceless millions.

### Sister and Whore

As Ray probes the contexts that have shaped Siddhartha's hesitancies, he takes us into the heart of the bourgeois world—the middle-class home—without idealizing it as a haven of Bengali values within the corrupt metropolis. Instead, he focuses on a typical middle-class crisis in which the family's respectability is at stake and the offender is a woman—sister Sutapa, who is evidently having an affair with her boss. Sexual taint brings maximum shame to a bourgeois household, and the mother is utterly distraught by the accusations leveled at her "respectable" daughter, which by qualification extend to her. Daughters are expected to guard their reputation and give no cause for their mothers to weep. But not only does Sutapa violate this dictum—even worse, she is quite unfazed by the charges or the fact that they leave her mother deeply hurt. "She'll get used to it," breezily she tells Siddhartha. As the new career-driven woman whose amorality recalls that of Adinath, Sutapa threatens to upset the old order as well as the old hypocrisies. Ray's cohesive community based on old-fashioned family values is crumbling fast.

Perhaps more than anyone else in Ray's cinema, Sutapa embodies the woman of the '70s. A good-looking woman with material ambitions, she is bent on furthering her career, even if it means reciprocating the sexual advances of her boss. Ray refuses to turn her story into one of guilt and redemption; instead, Sutapa remains a strong-willed, independent woman to the end, without regrets for daring to be different. In her rejection of middle-class morality and the role created for her by her class, she introduces a brand of feminism that is new to Ray's cinema.

Ray repeatedly associates her with her dressing-table mirror in which she likes to gaze at herself. There is no guilt or self-effacing modesty about such self-indulgence, which often borders on exhibitionism. We learn that she wishes to be a model and that she is learning to dance—activities that alienate her further from her class but that manifest her confidence in her body and sexuality. The more we see her preening before the mirror and lolling on the bed (instead of helping with the housework like a dutiful daughter), the more her pleasure-and-ego-driven nature becomes evident.

Denied the good life by her stringent upbringing, Sutapa wants to get out of the middle-class rut. Like Adinath, she belongs to the new breed of doers—a pragmatist who cannot be bothered with too much thinking or moral compunctions. She likes to get what she wants and doesn't worry about the means. Moreover, the fact that she is the sole breadwinner of the family deeply empowers her. Her job is her passport to power, independence, money. Thus she seems a completely alien creature within the middle-class setup: The new, aggressive woman who challenges all the conventions of female propriety.

But while Ray admires her energy and ambition, he cannot ignore the ethical consequences of her choice. As a shrewd, manipulative opportunist willing to sacrifice her morals for a Rs200 increment offered by her boss, Sutapa also represents the debasement of the middle-class woman in the consumer marketplace. Her bid to define her newfound independence through money brings her close to prostitution. In *Jana Aranya* Ray will develop this issue at length; here he alludes to it by linking Sutapa to the prostitute Siddhartha visits.

Since we always see Sutapa in relation to her brother and often from his point of view, she comes to occupy a central place in the discourse on action, sexuality, and family that involves him intimately. Often, in these contexts, she serves to bring out his failings, hesitations, and sexual repressions.

We hear Naresh ask Siddhartha whether his male pride is hurt because his sister has a job and he does not. Even though Siddhartha will not admit to it, we know the reversal in power relations adds to his insecurity as well as gives him an inferiority complex. Sutapa proves that she can not only hold her own with any man, but perhaps better him at the game. In every way she seems stronger, resourceful, and more decisive than her vacillating brother. In fact, she is truly the "man of the house." Finding a job becomes all the more urgent for Siddhartha, because his sense of male superiority is under assault.

One way to disarm the threat is to act as protective big brother. When Siddhartha claims that he will beat up her boss, he seems motivated more by self-interest than moral outrage or family honor. But Sutapa sees through this pathetic attempt to regain lost authority: "The thought of you beating up someone makes me laugh," she says, knowing fully well his fatal hesitations in the face of action.

The other threat that Siddhartha faces from Sutapa is sexual in nature. It is ironic that he reacts angrily to a man giving his sister unsolicited sexual attention when he could be held guilty of the same. His evident pleasure in fixing his gaze on her is amply demonstrated in the film. As we watch her watching herself in the mirror, we see Siddhartha watching her as she arranges her sari, lets down her hair, and engages in one of her exhibitionistic reveries. Incest within a middle-class setting is considered the ultimate perversion, and yet in the context of bourgeois repression it seems quite plausible that the sexually stifled male should unconsciously project his desires onto his sister.

One could argue that Sutapa's assumption of the male role in the house generates a profound castration anxiety in Siddhartha. His incestuous longings only compound the crisis, since they produce terrible guilt. While, fascinated, he watches her, he secretly fears her for the sexual feelings and sense of disempowerment she generates in him. Siddhartha's strategy to overcome such anxiety is to unconsciously conflate her with the woman who fills him with moral revulsion—the prostitute—and thereby degrade her. As "prostitute" Sutapa ceases to be a threat, since she can be dismissed as corrupt and depraved.

The first scene between Siddhartha and Sutapa that takes place in her bedroom is mimicked in part by the scene between Siddhartha and the prostitute a little later in the film. As the nurse stands before her dressing-table mirror, loosens her hair, glances at her reflection, and finally undresses, we notice an instant correspondence with some of Sutapa's actions. In fact, there is the same exhibitionism that we had noticed earlier. What is important to remember is that both scenes are associated with Siddhartha's point of view and that *he* draws an analogy between the women that we in turn experience through his gaze. When the prostitute sheds her sari and appears in her underclothes, she seems to enact what Sutapa had only insinuated through the seductive rearranging of her sari in front of him. In other words, if his sister had engaged in a subtle form of foreplay, now the prostitute makes it real for him. When she asks for five minutes to freshen up and heads for the bathroom, the link with Sutapa is reinforced, because she had said and done the same. But the prostitute goes one step further: She asks Adinath to help her with her bra hook, and, as we know, it is at this point that Siddhartha snaps.

In Adinath, Siddhartha finds a surrogate who acts out his own fantasies about his sister. With the mirror so central in this scene, he projects Adinath as his double, engaged in the perverse that he can only imagine but never dare. And it makes him recoil and rush out of the room. Thus there is a symbolic exorcism of guilt as Siddhartha identifies Sutapa with the prostitute and transfers his disgust for a whore onto her. Sex with his sister may be a secret longing, but as a conscious thought it breeds terror in an inhibited man. But, to his great relief, he doesn't have to commit such an act—Adinath does it for him and in the process sets him free. And yet Siddhartha finally emerges as a loser, unable to directly negotiate with his incestuous feelings nor shed his timidity and engage sexually with the prostitute. When it comes to decisive action, he still backs off.

The second meeting with Sutapa is after this visit. As she strikes the same postures in front of her mirror and before his voyeuristic gaze, she tells him that as a model she would have no qualms about wearing a skimpy outfit. Although he pretends to be shocked, in a subsequent scene we see him fantasizing her as a glamorous, sexy model. Again, we sense an analogy being drawn: His sister's displaying her body in public is tantamount to the prostitute's selling hers. After all, both professions involve money, marketing, and merchandise (and Sutapa stresses the lucrative aspect of the business). The strong fascination with his sister as sex object continues in a dream in which he imagines her on the beach in a swimsuit.

In the next sequence, Siddhartha watches Sutapa demonstrate the dancing lessons she is taking by performing with an imaginary partner on the roof. Invariably, this leads him to fantasize her with a real-life partner, surrounded by real-life dancing couples. While his bourgeois sense of propriety seems outraged at this display of exhibitionism (which renders her cheap and vulgar), there is, as before, a simultaneous pleasure in fantasizing her with another man. When he imagines her lighting a cigarette and blowing smoke (a direct quote from his visit to the prostitute), the Bengali-bourgeois stereotype of the "fast girl"—no better than a slut—is invoked. Thus repeatedly Siddhartha displays a fascinating paradox: Secretly desiring his sister while turning her into a depraved object in order to free himself from guilt and anxiety.

Within this scenario Keya operates as the agent who restores "normalcy." She is everything that Sutapa is not: Asexual, nonaggressive, nonmaterialistic, and, above all, nonthreatening. In fact, she fits the prototype of the respectable middle-class woman with whom Siddhartha can feel "safe." By offering him her love and friendship, she delivers him from his incestuous passion, exorcises his guilt, and restores his tattered bourgeois self-confidence. We see a symbolic enactment of this process as she replaces Sutapa in the same dream in which the latter appears in a swimsuit.

The dream offers us a shorthand version of recent events in Siddhartha's life, some shot in negative and intercut with his reaction shots. We first see a beach (an allusion to Siddhartha's physical displacement, since there is no sea at Calcutta), bottled fetuses, an interview committee, Sutapa modeling in a swimsuit, a car being attacked by a mob. Some semblance of a narrative develops as a firing squad takes aim and shoots dead Tunu. As Siddhartha looks on, Sutapa in a nurse's uniform bends over the corpse. There is a sudden switch in identity and Sutapa becomes Keya. The dream ends with a puzzled Siddhartha asking Keya, "It's you?"

The dream, then, originates as an anxiety dream strewn with emblems of Siddhartha's guilt, insecurity, confusion, and failure. Sutapa in swimsuit is both allure and threat; the car recalls the mob lynching and his inability to act; the committee (in negative) points to his failed interview at the start of the film. The sequence of shots relating to Tunu, several of which are also in negative, features Siddhartha's projections of what he could have been and what he lacks. Tunu's heroics—smiling defiantly at the moment of death—are alien to a "thinker" like him. There is also a death wish here—to die more meaningfully than he has lived. Since Tunu's execution comes immediately after the shot of Sutapa in her swimsuit, perhaps the wish has its source in sexual guilt as well. The bottled fetuses—more allusions to death—confirm this feeling of a wasted life, of lost potential. At the same time, the frozen embryos perhaps hold out hope of a birth, or rebirth—just as does the presence of the sea in the background.

Tunu's death marks the turning point of this anxiety dream as it brings together the three women who have recently figured in Siddhartha's life. In a neat compression, the swimsuit-clad Sutapa, who embodies his incestuous desire and guilt, becomes, in her nurse's uniform, equated with the whore. She is the "bad" nurse who ministers to the baser needs of her "patients" and engenders disgust in Siddhartha. As she is replaced by Keya, also in a nurse's uniform, there is amazement and relief on Siddhartha's face, since the "good" nurse has appeared to "cure" his sickness. Thus Keya successfully displaces both Sutapa and the whore and defines her place in his life. He awakens from this exorcism with a new sense of her role in his existence. But Ray doesn't want us to forget that as a wish-fulfillment dream it shows Siddhartha once again fleeing from his anxieties instead of confronting them. What is more, by turning Keya into his source of salvation, he makes her bear the burden of his failures. All he *does* in the dream is stand by passively and observe others engage in action. His only gesture of approval is directed at the woman who acts on *his behalf* while he remains frozen in immobility.

### The Decisive Moment

Ray, as we have seen, does not treat Siddhartha's waiting in the margins as a dead-end condition. Even Siddhartha's passive observation of the world is paradoxically an active process, since it also, like everything else in his life, will shape his choice. Nothing, for Ray, exists in isolation, and Siddhartha's decision to act at the end serves as a cumulative gesture. To translate a lifetime's worth of experience into action calls for a trigger that the interview at the end of the film will offer Siddhartha.

There are two interviews in *Pratidwandi*, and, like the allusions to death, they come respectively at the beginning and end of the film. Not only do they serve to highlight the reality of joblessness within the modern bourgeois nation, but point to the failure of the state in resolving the problem. In the process, they portray a bureaucracy that is cold, callous, and absurd. But, even more important, they draw attention to the victims of the rat race who find themselves playing a role in an elaborate farce.

When Siddhartha is asked during the first interview to define the most outstanding event of the last decade, he opts for the war in Vietnam, and is immediately asked whether he considers it more significant than the moon landing. When he speaks of the "extraordinary power of resistance" displayed by the Vietnamese people, he is asked whether he is a communist. Siddhartha's reply—"One doesn't have to be one to admire Vietnam"—only fuels their paranoia of a subversive infiltrating the establishment. The moon landing is apolitical, safe, and all the more reassuring, since it invokes Western capitalism and technology. Siddhartha is abruptly told to leave. Integrity doesn't count in the rat race we hear him tell a friend later—one must learn to pander and please.

Ray painstakingly sets up the second interview to expose its even more perverse nature. Seventy-five applicants have been called to fill four vacancies. Each interview, we learn, will last about three minutes at first, then get shorter and shorter in length. The questions have virtually no relevance to contemporary India. There is a strong suspicion that the jobs are already earmarked for inside candidates.

The seventy-five bravely sweat it out on a hot day under two fans, of which only one is working (there are repeated allusions to the lack of air in the film). Most stand, since only a few chairs have been provided (there is a scramble as soon as a seat is vacated, mirroring the politics of the rat race). As cigarette butts proliferate in a sand bucket we sense the terrible sameness all around. At the same time, as Ray picks out faces, we are reminded of each person's uniqueness. However, it's only a momentary reprieve—the sheer numbers threaten to render them all faceless.

Siddhartha watches, squeezed in between two walls, next to a poster appropriately about "Strikers" and "Nonstrikers." Within this middle space we sense his growing alienation, his anger slowly building up. When a man topples over and faints he cannot stay aloof any longer. As he leads a small delegation inside to protest the appalling

conditions, we sense an identification with the crowd. No longer
intimidated by their anonymity, he sees himself as one of them, and
there is a genuine concern for this community of strangers united by
hope and despair.

Inside, they are met with hostility and indifference. When
Siddhartha is singled out for a personal attack, he defends himself by
invoking the group: "I haven't come here to talk about myself." At
that moment, the men turn tail and disappear through the door, leaving him alone. They cannot meet his gaze when he joins them outside. As the camera pans over their faces, we see them no longer as
people with separate identities but more as a shapeless blur. Incapable
of protesting their indignities, they lose their chance to become faces
and bodies capable of defining themselves as individuals within a collective. Their failure to act cohesively echoes their larger failure
within a faction-ridden nation governed by self-interest.

Back in his corner, as Siddhartha tilts back his head and closes
his eyes, we see the images that appear on his mindscreen: A beggar,
a slum, a bunch of hippies, people eating in an affluent house, a
stretch of road. Although these remembered strands lack a coherent
pattern, they constitute in outline his wandering street life. More significantly, they suggest "the polarities between wealth and power that
he is sensitive to."[7] They prove our earlier hypothesis to be wrong—
his snapshot views of the world have been more than mere cursory
glances at a reality he felt too diffident to engage with. What he saw
remains and festers within, and it fuels his rage.

When Siddhartha opens his eyes most of the men have wilted in
the heat and begun to doze. As he looks at them, he dissects them
with his X-ray vision into a set of skeletons that not only display an
appalling sameness, but embody the most extreme form imaginable
of dehumanization. The vision gives way to a shot of Siddhartha's
angry face. It is at this point that the committee announces a lunch
break. It is the last straw for him. Striding into the room, his anger
explodes: "Are we animals? What right have you to treat us like this?
. . . I want an answer." Precisely because nobody has ever given him

an answer nor can provide him with one now, Siddhartha uses his hands and body to make a statement. He throws ink on the wall, overturns a table, hurls a chair, shoves aside a man who tries to stop him. Done with language, lies, silence, and waiting, he frames a gesture through his direct physical intervention. The sequence ends with a shot of a lighted table lamp on the floor—Apu's lamp of learning and progress.

For most critics, Siddhartha's one-man protest amounts to little because it accomplishes nothing concrete. For Das Gupta, it is an "an act of courage" that "is fruitless in the outcome."[8] While Philip Kemp concedes that it is "psychologically cathartic," he also points out that "nothing has been changed, no enlightenment achieved."[9] Nyce informs us that in India, the ending was criticized even more sharply by radicals who felt that the logical arena for Siddhartha's growth should be "political activism."[10] Instead, Ray suggested that such growth could only occur in "a private region."[11] Nyce adds that "the film presents in compelling detail all the reasons for radical politics and then rejects those politics."[12]

In reply, Ray makes a distinction between "emotional gestures" and "ideological gestures" and indicates his preference for the former.[13] What appeals to him most is that Siddhartha carries out an act of protest "on a personal level, which to me is a marvelous thing because it comes from inside and not as an expression of a political ideology."[14] For him, the right choices are determined by one's inner groping and searching. There is a whole life behind Siddhartha's act, a whole spectrum of deeply felt experience along with a festering anger at a corrupt system. His outburst is not merely a calculated political gesture but a supremely individual one, backed by thought and feeling. It is political in a larger sense because it involves a whole sensibility and way of life. In contrast, Tunu's planned, ideological violence is less authentic. Thus Ray applauds the power and integrity of such a profoundly personal gesture. For him, political change happens slowly, but only through such acts of courage—both big and small—that bear out the inner convictions of the doer. Siddhartha is a better man for having dared, for finally having broken out of his apathy. Although banished to a small town and to the margins again, he has successfully redefined his psychic territory and relocated himself within a new center. And this newfound sense of place is vindicated as he hears the bird call from his childhood.

## The Bird Call

After the antipastoralism of *Aranyer Din Ratri*, Ray indulges in a spurt of romanticism in *Pratidwandi* as he turns to Siddhartha's memory of a sylvan world haunted by the call of a strange bird. This prelapsarian Eden in flashback is meant to serve as a foil to the urban squalor in the film, but it seems a bit trite, a cliché at best. This is the last time in the Calcutta films that Ray evokes nature before the world of concrete and glass closes in on his protagonists.

For Siddhartha, the bird "evokes the feeling of wonder, of the potentiality of life, of first sight and first hearing."[15] He associates it with his childhood, with a holiday outside Calcutta during a time of innocence and bonding. We see the three siblings happily gamboling along without a care in the world. Sutapa, who first hears the bird, asks him to listen to its call; he, in turn, asks his servant—in Hindi—to identify it. It is significant that the bird belongs to a place far removed from Siddhartha's daily urban world and that he can experience such an epiphany only here, where he is spatially and linguistically displaced from the familiar. Since he never hears the bird again nor finds out its name, it becomes a symbol of a magical world from which he feels increasingly cut off in a cold and changed present. As his urban alienation intensifies, so does his search for the bird.

But a bird call and not the chant of revolution? How do we account for Siddhartha's excessive investment in nostalgia, in something so "impractical" when there are more urgent problems to be addressed? Is this a display of bourgeois self-indulgence as Tunu seems to suggest? It would be easy to condemn him as politically irresponsible, but what is also apparent here is his profound sensitivity and imagination. The bird call alludes to a part of him that we know is vital to his overall sense of self. Thus identified, the bird figures crucially in Siddhartha's decision to act.

There is a special relevance to the fact that Sutapa triggers Siddhartha's first flashback about the bird in the film—she who has changed so radically. Neither she nor Tunu display any nostalgia for the past. For them, "the mysterious magic of memory means nothing at all." [16] Siddhartha recalls another bird from presumably the same holiday—a chicken that was decapitated right before their eyes. While he had turned away, Tunu had watched with fascination. Ray juxtaposes both birds—one remains invisible and sings, the other dies horribly, struggling—within Siddhartha's memory to define the two different facets of his sensitivity. And he shows how, unlike Tunu and Sutapa, his "childhood is still alive" within him. [17]

After he meets Keya the bird becomes associated with her in the same dream in which she tends to the dying Tunu. As she raises her head to return Siddhartha's gaze, we see birds fly across her face, accompanied by the call of the bird. Siddhartha seems to locate in Keya's compassionate, caring nature something of the bird's transcendental quality. When it reappears at the end of the film, it once again is linked to Keya as he describes the bird to her in a letter he is composing in his head. She is the only one who would understand. As bird and Keya come together through these two references, we realize how getting to know her has brought Siddhartha closer to finding his bird.

When Siddhartha finally hears the bird call, it is in the small town in the Hindi-speaking belt where once again he has become displaced. Physically dislocated from the city he loves and hates and separated from the woman he cares for, Siddhartha is out of sync with his world. But the bird call becomes a sign of a deeper inner accomplishment. In a sense, it becomes a vindication of what he has achieved through the choice he has made. Siddhartha may have lost out to the city and to Tunu's notion of political change, but he has gained within. And at this moment of self-growth and revival the bird sings to him. Freed from the malaise of the city, he regains a lost link with nature that will revitalize him. The bird sings, forming "a bridge across time and space."[18]

But Ray doesn't end the film on such a smug note. He juxtaposes the bird call with a funeral chant. From Siddhartha's hotel balcony we see a funeral procession in the distance. The chant is in Hindi and it reminds us of Siddhartha's exile, his return to new, unfamiliar borders. Also, the allusion to death takes us back to the start of the film, where we witnessed his father's death—the source of a profound dislocation in him. Now as bird call merges with funeral chant, opposites are reconciled within a dynamic fusion. As Nyce explains: "Something is dying in him and something is being reborn."[19] Siddhartha's "death" has led to a symbolic rebirth away from the city, and the bird's call heralds it. The last shot is a freeze of him turning slowly to the camera; suspended out of time—as in his many flashbacks and fantasies—within the quasi-mystical space of an epiphany, he rises above the quotidian and communes with the timeless.

## Notes

1. Samik Bandyopadhyay, "Introduction," in *Satyajit Ray: A Film by Shyam Benegal*, ed. Alakananda Datta and Samik Bandyopadhyay (Calcutta: Seagull Books, 1988), vi.

2. Alan Ross, "Goodbye to Calcutta." *Telegraph Sunday Magazine* (Calcutta) (July 3, 1983): 11.

3. Christian Braad Thomsen, "Ray's New Trilogy." *Sight and Sound* 42, no. 1 (1972–73): 33.

4. Tom Milne, "*The Adversary*." *Sight and Sound* 42, no. 2 (1973): 111.

5. Udayan Gupta, "The Politics of Humanism." *Cineaste* 12, no. 1 (1982): 27.

6. Ibid., 27.

7. Ben Nyce, *Satyajit Ray: A Study of His Films* (New York: Praeger, 1988), 132.

8. Chidananda Das Gupta, *The Cinema of Satyajit Ray* (New Delhi: National Book Trust, 1994), 95.

9. Philip Kemp, "Satyajit Ray," in *World Film Directors*, Vol. II, ed. John Wakeman (New York: H. W. Wilson, 1988), 848.

10. Nyce, *Satyajit Ray*, 133.
11. Ibid., 133.
12. Ibid., 133.
13. Thomsen, "Ray's New Trilogy," 33.
14. Ibid., 33.
15. Nyce, *Satyajit Ray*, 133.
16. Milne, "*The Adversary*," 111.
17. Nyce, *Satyajit Ray*, 133.
18. Milne, "*The Adversary*," 111.
19. Nyce, *Satyajit Ray*, 133.

# Conclusion

**F**rom Apu learning to write in
*Pather Panchali* to Siddhartha's
crisis of choice in *Pratidwandi*, it is possible to trace the trajectory of
Ray's modernity as it evolves from an enlightened humanist's faith
in progress to the gradual erosion of that faith. Within that trajectory,
as this book has tried to show, he seeks to describe the sociocultural
formation of a nation and its identity. For Ray, what makes India distinctively modern is its hybrid nature, its ability to assimilate divergent influences and reinvent itself while remaining thoroughly
"Indian." The contexts that he emphasizes in his films are now
familiar to us: The dynamics of an East–West collision; the advent of
urban culture and technology; the importance of education, writing,
and language; the evolution of new forms of human subjectivity; the
solidarity of the family threatened by a reformulation of traditional

beliefs and gender roles; the new place of the individual and his inevitable sense of dislocation in a world of change; the search for independence by women within a patriarchal society, which is often feudal in outlook; the crisis of values in the morally bankrupt India of the '70s; and the subsequent selling of India—reinscribed in English—to the West.

While such contexts provide a sense of Ray's involvement with the modern, they also prompt the question: How modern is Ray's modernity? The question becomes all the more pertinent when one considers his lifelong relationship to the nineteenth century and his commitment to values that he described as "timeless" and "universal."[1] In his later years the question was broached more frequently by his detractors, who felt that Ray's cinema had lost all relevance. Even the films that sought to grapple with India's post–Independence problems, they argued, were essentially bourgeois and conservative. Lacking any real knowledge of modern industrial society, Ray was incapable of bringing out "all the nuances, the shades of irony, the ambiguities, and, above all, the mind-boggling complexities of modern urban existence."[2] In short, Ray's modernity was much too traditional to truly embrace the contemporary.

Much of the criticism leveled at Ray revolves around a fixed set of issues. For many, he remained a neorealist at heart whose espousal of realism was part of an old-fashioned humanist agenda that he would have done well to discard. Such critics tend to ignore the major shifts in Ray's career, his choice of diverse subjects and historical periods or the fact that he tried his hand at a wide range of genres that included the musical and the fantasy film (*Goopy Gyne Bagha Byne/The Adventures of Goopy and Bagha*, 1969, and *Hirak Rajar Deshe/The Kingdom of Diamonds*, 1980). The same critics tend to underplay the stylistic innovations that surfaced in his work—especially the disjunctive aesthetic of the jump cut that *Pratidwandi* inaugurated. Such experiments with form, they claim, did not generate a new cinematic discourse, since Ray's cinema at heart would remain committed to realism, narrative, and a value system that looked back to the humanistic ideals of the Bengali Renaissance. They point to the fact that Ray displayed his impatience with the experiments of the Indian New Wave during the '70s by criticizing a certain film-maker's "plain lack of interest in human beings."[3] It was clearly difficult for him to identify with a cinema that broke away from the principles that governed his own.

Ray's political conservatism, according to his Marxist critics, is another serious obstacle to his growth as a modern artist. For them, he is a bourgeois at heart, unable to make a stand or subscribe to a specific ideology. They single out in particular his philosophical detachment, his aesthetics of contemplation, and his investment in irony, all of which prevent him from directly engaging with urgent social and political problems. They also identify his career-long obsession with the middle class as a sign of his inability to grapple with social realities other than his own. Specifically, they question the absence from his cinema of the disenfranchised masses of India.

For such critics, Ray's claim that he is committed to man[4] relates to an outdated, bourgeois humanism. They question the progressive agenda of the Bengali Renaissance and the emancipatory vision of humanity that he imbibed from it. It is true that in Ray's early work there is a preference for multiple points of view, an insistence on the many-sidedness of life, and a reluctance to judge and condemn. His human subjects are viewed more as people of diverse dispositions who have their reasons for behaving the way they do, rather than as individuals who are simply good or bad. As fully rounded characters, they always retain a sense of their potential as human beings. This explains the relative absence of outright villains in these films, which has led to comparisons with Renoir and an assumption that Ray believed in the essential goodness of his protagonists. In reality, there are plenty of unsavory characters in this phase of his work but they come across as confused, vacillating, misguided individuals who could surely be repatriated to society with a good dose of education and a firm appeal to reason. For his detractors, such idealism, especially in the context of contemporary India, seems dangerously naive.

Demanding a more stridently political approach, Ray's critics in the '70s asked for a cinema that would emphasize social and historical subjects, define ideological frameworks, and offer an agenda for change. Ray was much too concerned with specific individuals and their specific problems, they complained, to provide an analysis of the ideological factors that shape lives. Even when he focused on history, it served mostly as a backdrop to the human drama. Thus the most crucial issues got deflected as they were filtered through his human agents. What was needed instead was a strong critique of the social and political mechanisms of oppression within an unjust system. Ray would have to take an ideological stand on the post–Independence, post–Tagorean world and offer a truly contemporary perspective instead of a moralistic nineteenth-century point of view.

Those who defend Ray from such charges of bourgeois complacency often refer to his stark depiction of poverty and human misery in *Pather Panchali*. But this rarely appeases his detractors, who feel he doesn't show enough. Moreover, his understated poetic realism, they argue, is hopelessly incompatible with the politics of hunger. If such a representation is to be forceful, then it should be backed by a proper evaluation of the political and economic factors that cause hunger. They also find fault with Ray's celebration of a preindustrial innocence in the film, finding it romantic and irresponsible. Why doesn't Ray focus more on the political realities of pre–Independence rural India, which featured not only hunger, but casteism, communalism, and the exploitation of landlords? The film, they claim, offers a highly subjective and incomplete rendition of history. As one critic puts it, *Pather Panchali* is "a romantic idealization of village life, even with all its attendant ills."[5] (Similar charges were leveled at *Ashani Sanket/Distant Thunder* [1973], a film about the 1943 man-made Bengal famine. Ray was accused of making the famine look too beautiful by shooting it in color and by keeping the horrors of starvation mostly offscreen.)

This raises the question of how "authentic" is Ray's India? Das Gupta complained in the '60s that the Calcutta of the burning trams was absent from Ray's cinema.[6] One could add other omissions such as inner-city life, urban squalor, the abuse of minorities, slum life, domestic and political violence. To dismiss Ray on such grounds as being morally and politically irresponsible would be doing him a grave injustice. An artist is under no compulsion to include all aspects of a specific reality. He clearly has a right to his own subjectivity. Ray makes up for what he omits with other subjects that are socially and politically pertinent. This fact cannot be disputed, even if his critics may disagree as to the nature and effectiveness of his representation. However, at the same time, it is true that the India Ray describes betrays his own bourgeois affiliations, since it caters largely to the interests of his class. More important than the question of authenticity, then, is the question of how *representative* is Ray's India? For an artist who seeks to define the emergence of a new nation, the question is a vital one.

The evolution of Ray's cinema proves that he was not only aware of his critics but also sought to answer many of their charges. The most radical shift in his work, as we have seen, came in the '70s with *Aranyer Din Ratri* and the Calcutta trilogy. As the ideological foundations of his world were eroded in the post–Nehruvian era, Ray's project of "affirming the human"[7] proved more and more problematic. *Aranyer Din Ratri* initiated his first major revaluation of humanism with its depiction of four good-for-nothing city slickers. The antihumanism of the film is felt not only in the way it exposes the inadequacies of the men, but also by the fact that it makes them seem incapable of any redemption. In *Seemabaddha/Company Limited* (1971) and *Jana Aranya/The Middle Man* (1975), the two films that along with *Pratidwandi* comprise the Calcutta trilogy, there is a similar lack of hope at the end. Both protagonists become casualties of the rat race as they betray their morals for the sake of their careers. In *Seemabaddha* the successful company executive engages in fraud to ensure his own promotion as director of his firm. In *Jana Aranya* the protagonist has to provide his client with a prostitute—his best friend's sister—to win a lucrative contract. Ray doesn't allow these men even the redemptive gesture with which Siddhartha defines himself at the end of *Pratidwandi*. There is only a sense of profound loss and guilt.

Such scenarios will recur as Ray increasingly offers us men and women who are confused, unhappy, and often corrupt. Perhaps the most extreme example of this trend can be found in *Shatranj ki Khilari/The Chess Players* (1977) where, in a scathing attack on feudalism, Ray portrays a pair of dysfunctional noblemen. Utterly devoted to playing chess, they pay no heed to the British marching in and annexing their kingdom. Ray follows this up a few films later with *Sadgati/Deliverance* (1981), which features a fully formed symbol of malevolence—a Brahmin priest whose utter heartlessness causes the death of an Untouchable. In creating an unmitigated villain, more ruthless than even his critics could imagine, Ray lays to rest the charge of subscribing to an unreal, facile humanism.

Such a bleak sense of human potential is supported by Ray's overall sense of political doom. During the making of *Jana Aranya*, he confessed that he felt abject despair all around him, with no possible solution in sight.[8] Indeed, the film is his most tragic, a poignant admission that his cherished values of the Tagorean ethos are truly dead. The credits, in fact, appear over students who openly cheat during their B.A. exams. Later in the film we encounter some of the familiar subjects of the Calcutta trilogy—corruption, unemployment, prostitution—but on an unprecedented scale. In this respect the film goes much further than *Aranyer Din Ratri* and *Pratidwandi*, announcing the end of a whole vision of life in which education heralded progress and emancipation.

Although Ray never made the kind of film his Marxist critics urged him to make, he would now give more space to the political in his work. It also accounts for a branching out in search of new subjects and social groups who had not appeared in his films before. By making an Untouchable the protagonist of *Sadgati*, Ray disproved the label of being a bourgeois filmmaker. Among his unrealized projects were a documentary on child labor and a feature film on tribals. Toward the end of his life, it seems, he was all set to offer a more inclusive and integrated version of India. It would have been yet another rejoinder to his critics.

It is tempting to read such developments as evidence of a new radical modernity in Ray's work. However, it would be more appropriate to refer to a new, complex, and *larger* sense of the modern. Despite all the changes we have noticed and despite the despairing vision of *Jana Aranya*, Ray remained faithful to many of his earlier assumptions. For example, he never lost his fascination with human beings, even when they appeared deeply flawed. The individual remained at the center of his cinema. In fact, in Ray's last three films there is a return to the old vindication of human potential, focusing once again on people who in the face of isolation and rejection hold onto their integrity. In *Ganashatru/An Enemy of the People* (1989), based on Ibsen's play, an honest doctor is spurned by his community; in *Shakha Proshakha/Branches of a Tree* (1990) the mad son in the family proves to be the most wise and sane; in *Agantuk/The Stranger* (1991) an outsider intrudes on a bourgeois family and teaches them some fundamental truths about life and living. Like Tagore, Ray refused to lose faith in man.

Despite shifting gears in the '70s, Ray continued to maintain his political obliqueness. In the Calcutta trilogy he refrains from defining political parties, politicians, and agendas by name. In *Pratidwandi* he does not divulge Tunu's identity as a Naxalite, even though it is obvious to his viewers. Our sense that something is deeply wrong with this society evolves out of our direct experience of the film, since Ray never engages in any form of rhetoric. He prefers to maintain a certain ahistoricity within the historical framework of his film.

His refusal to endorse any kind of collective political action or offer us some vision of reform at the close of these films does not surprise us. Ray's deep distrust of utopias, agendas, ideologies, and revolutions remains to the end. In this respect he lives up to his reputation for being politically conservative. Ray's individuals, pitted against the faceless structures of postindustrial bureaucracy, have recourse only to gestures that define them as worthy human beings but do not resolve their conflicts. We see this repeatedly in Ray's work—a turning away from political action and from the public domain to the private, intimate space of the individual desperately trying to formulate a significant mode of action. Hence the charge that Ray's middle-class diffidence prevents him from offering a truly radical agenda for change.

Ray also maintained—despite all the cynicism of his middle and last phases—his faith in certain values that he considered timeless and universal. However culture-specific human existence is, he believed that people are governed by certain fundamentals that are cross-cultural. Gaston Roberge speaks of Ray's attempt to affirm "the universal essence"[9] of man within his social and political existence. Ray's films from the start show a preoccupation with moral and ethical issues, an insistence on the value of truth, an investment in hope in the face of despair, as well as a belief in the triumph of goodness, integrity, and justice. Similarly, he upholds the importance of family and community. What makes his position problematic is his faith in the *perennial* relevance of these issues. In reality, many of Ray's "timeless" values were of nineteenth-century vintage.

Ray's sense of the modern therefore cannot be understood in terms of a rupture with the past. Instead, there is always a sense of accommodation—of the new incorporating the old, the past existing within the present. His modernity is one of synthesis, of reconciliation and acceptance, of bringing together diverse strands of experience that may at first seem incompatible. Instead of a fixed and inert sense of the modern, then, we have the notion of an evolving process that incorporates a wide range of disparate elements and constantly redefines itself.

The idea of a blend, of opposites forming a relationship is dramatized at the end of *Apur Sansar* as Apu walks away with his son on his shoulders against the reassuring vista of timeless, rural India. Having made a strong case for modernity all along, the trilogy ends unexpectedly with a strong affirmation of traditional values. Ray upholds all that is perennial in the Indian way of life, including its deeply nourishing philosophy of salvation through pain. The city, in fact, seems to lose out—the site of solitude, grief, dislocation. Ray's abrupt turnaround only confirms his sense of the modern as a discourse that must necessarily encompass highly divergent and contradictory experiences. Such a notion of inclusivity, as we have seen, forms the basis for his vision of a hybrid, pluralistic nation. Within the wide horizons of his cinematic universe there is always room for everyone and for all things.

## Notes

1. Satyajit Ray, "Under Western Eyes." *Sight and Sound* 51, no. 4 (1982): 274.

2. Soumitro Das, "Blinkers on the Inner Eye." *Telegraph* (Calcutta) (January 24, 1994): 6.

3. Satyajit Ray, "Four and a Quarter," in *Our Films Their Films* (Hyderabad: Orient Longman, 1993), 105.

4. Karuna Shankar Roy, "The Artist in Politics: An Interview with Satyajit Ray." *Drama Review* 15, no. 2 (1971): 310.

5. John W. Hood, *Time and Dreams: The Films of Buddhadeb Dasgupta* (Calcutta: Seagull Books, 1998), 61.

6. Das Gupta, Chidananda. "Ray and Tagore." *Sight and Sound* 36, no. 1 (1966–67): 30–34.

7. Gaston Roberge, "Satyajit Ray: Humanism in the Cinema," in *Satyajit Ray Retrospective Souvenir: The Second Decade*, ed. Swapan Majumdar (Calcutta: n.p., 1979), n.p.

8. Andrew Robinson, *Satyajit Ray: The Inner Eye* (Berkeley: University of California Press, 1989), 207.

9. Roberge, "Satyajit Ray," n.p.

# Chronology

**1921**   Ray is born in Calcutta on May 2, the son of Sukumar and Suprabha Ray

**1923**   Sukumar Ray dies

**1929**   Enrolls in Ballygunge Government High School

**1936**   Finishes school. Joins Presidency College. Wins first prize in a photographic contest organized by *Boy's Own Paper*

**1940**   Graduates with honors in economics from Presidency College. Enrolls in fine arts at Visva Bharati University, Shantiniketan

**1943**   Back in Calcutta, joins D. J. Keymer, a British advertising agency, as a commercial artist

**1945**   Illustrates an abridged edition of *Pather Panchali*

**1947**   Starts the Calcutta Film Society with Chidananda Das Gupta

**1949**   Marries Bijoya Das
Meets Renoir in Calcutta

**1950**  Spends six months in London. Sees *Bicycle Thief*

**1953**  Birth of son Sandip

**1955**  *Pather Panchali* is released in Calcutta

**1956**  *Pather Panchali* wins Best Human Document Award at the Cannes Film Festival

**1957**  *Aparajito* wins the Golden Lion of St. Mark at the Venice Film Festival

**1960**  Death of Suprabha Ray

**1964**  *Mahanagar* wins the Silver Bear for Best Direction at the Berlin Film Festival

**1965**  *Charulata* wins the Silver Bear for Best Direction at the Berlin Film Festival

**1974**  *Ashani Sanket* wins the Golden Bear at the Berlin Film Festival
D. Litt. from the Royal College of Arts, London

**1976**  Publication of *Our Films Their Films*

**1978**  D. Litt from Oxford University, England
Special Award, Berlin Film Festival

**1979**  Special Award, Moscow Film Festival

**1982**  "Hommage á Satyajit Ray," Cannes Film Festival. The festival awards him the Headless Angel Trophy
Special Golden Lion of St. Mark, Venice Film Festival

**1983**  Fellowship of the British Film Institute

**1987**  Legion d'Honneur from France

**1992**  Oscar for Lifetime Achievement
Dies in Calcutta on April 23

**1998**  Posthumously awarded the Bharat Ratna by the Government of India

# Filmography

**1955**

*Pather Panchali (Song of the Little Road)*

|   |   |
|---|---|
| Producer: | Government of West Bengal |
| Screenplay: | Satyajit Ray (based on the novel *Pather Panchali* by Bibhuti Bhusan Banerjee) |
| Photography: | Subrata Mitra |
| Music: | Ravi Shankar |
| Cast: | Kanu Banerjee, Karuna Banerjee, Subir Banerjee, Uma Das Gupta, Chunibala Devi |
| Length: | 115 minutes |

**1956**

*Aparajito (The Unvanquished)*

|   |   |
|---|---|
| Producer: | Epic Films |
| Screenplay: | Satyajit Ray (based on the novel *Aparajito* by Bibhuti Bhusan Banerjee) |
| Photography: | Subrata Mitra |
| Music: | Ravi Shankar |
| Cast: | Kanu Banerjee, Karuna Banerjee, Pinaki Sen Gupta, Smaran Ghosal |
| Length: | 113 minutes |

## 1957

*Parash Pathar (The Philosopher's Stone)*

Producer: Promod Lahiri
Screenplay: Satyajit Ray (based on the short story "Parash Pathar" by Parasuram)
Photography: Subrata Mitra
Music: Ravi Shankar
Cast: Tulsi Chakravarti, Ranibala, Kali Banerjee, Gangapada Bose
Length: 111 minutes

## 1958

*Jalsaghar (The Music Room)*

Producer: Satyajit Ray Productions
Screenplay: Satyajit Ray (based on the short story "Jalsaghar" by Tarasankar Banerjee)
Photography: Subrata Mitra
Music: Vilayat Khan
Cast: Chhabi Biswas, Padma Devi, Pinaki Sen Gupta, Gangapada Bose
Length: 100 minutes

## 1959

*Apur Sansar (The World of Apu)*

Producer: Satyajit Ray Productions
Screenplay: Satyajit Ray (based on the novel *Aparajito* by Bibhuti Bhusan Banerjee)
Photography: Subrata Mitra
Music: Ravi Shankar
Cast: Soumitra Chatterjee, Sharmila Tagore, Alok Chakravarti, Swapan Mukherjee
Length: 106 minutes

## 1960

*Devi (The Goddess)*

|  |  |
|---|---|
| Producer: | Satyajit Ray Productions |
| Screenplay: | Satyajit Ray (based on the short story "Devi" by Prabhat Kumar Mukherjee) |
| Photography: | Subrata Mitra |
| Music: | Ravi Shankar |
| Cast: | Chhabi Biswas, Soumitra Chatterjee, Sharmila Tagore, Purnendu Mukherjee, Karuna Banerjee |
| Length: | 93 minutes |

## 1961

*Teen Kanya (Three Daughters)*

|  |  |
|---|---|
| Producer: | Satyajit Ray Productions |
| Screenplay: | Satyajit Ray (based on three short stories by Rabindranath Tagore) |
| Photography: | Soumendu Roy |
| Music: | Satyajit Ray |
| Cast: | *The Postmaster*: Anil Chatterjee, Chandana Banerjee. *Monihara (The Lost Jewels)*: Kali Banerjee, Kanika Majumdar, Kumar Roy. *Samapti (The Conclusion)*: Soumitra Chatterjee, Aparna Das Gupta, Sita Mukherjee |
| Length: | 173 minutes |

## 1961

*Rabindranath Tagore*

|  |  |
|---|---|
| Producer: | Films Division, Government of India. |
| Script and Commentary: | Satyajit Ray |
| Photography: | Soumendu Roy |
| Music: | Jyotirindra Moitra |
| Cast: | Raya Chatterjee, Sovanlal Ganguli, Smaran Ghosal, Purnendu Mukherjee |
| Length: | 54 minutes |

**1962**

*Kanchanjungha*

>            Producer:  N.C.A. Productions
>          Screenplay:  Satyajit Ray
>        Photography:  Subrata Mitra
>               Music:  Satyajit Ray
>                 Cast:  Chhabi Biswas, Karuna Banerjee, Anubha Gupta, Subrata
>                         Sen, Alaknanda Roy, Arun Mukherjee, N. Viswanathan,
>                         Pahari Sanyal
>              Length:  120 minutes

**1962**

*Abhijan (The Expedition)*

>            Producer:  Abhijatrik
>          Screenplay:  Satyajit Ray (based on the novel *Abhijan* by Tarasankar
>                         Banerjee)
>        Photography:  Soumendu Roy
>               Music:  Satyajit Ray
>                 Cast:  Soumitra Chatterjee, Waheeda Rehman, Ruma Guha
>                         Thakurta, Ganesh Mukherjee, Rabi Ghosh
>              Length:  150 minutes

**1963**

*Mahanagar (The Big City)*

>            Producer:  R.D.B. and Co.
>          Screenplay:  Satyajit Ray (based on the short story "Abataranika" by
>                         Narendranath Mitra)
>        Photography:  Subrata Mitra
>               Music:  Satyajit Ray
>                 Cast:  Anil Chatterjee, Madhabi Mukherjee, Jaya Bhaduri,
>                         Haradhan Bnaerjee
>              Length:  131 minutes

**1964**

*Charulata*

| | |
|---|---|
| Producer: | R.D.B. and Co. |
| Screenplay: | Satyajit Ray (based on the novella "Nastanirh" by Rabindranath Tagore) |
| Photography: | Subrata Mitra |
| Music: | Satyajit Ray |
| Cast: | Soumitra Chatterjee, Madhabi Mukherjee, Sailen Mukherjee, Shyamal Ghosal, Gitali Roy |
| Length: | 117 minutes |

**1964**

*Two*

| | |
|---|---|
| Producer: | Esso World Theater |
| Screenplay: | Satyajit Ray |
| Photography: | Soumendu Roy |
| Music: | Satyajit Ray |
| Cast: | Ravi Kiran |
| Length: | 15 minutes |

**1965**

*Kapurush-O-Mahapurush (The Coward and the Holy Man)*

| | |
|---|---|
| Producer: | R.D.B. and Co. |
| Screenplay: | Satyajit Ray (based on the short stories "Janaiko Kapuruser Kahini" by Premendra Mitra and "Birinchi Baba" by Parasuram) |
| Photography: | Soumendu Roy |
| Music: | Satyajit Ray |
| Cast: | *Kapurush*: Soumitra Chatterjee, Madhabi Mukherjee, Haradhan Banerjee. *Mahapurush*: Charuprakash Ghosh, Rabi Ghosh, Satindra Bhattacharya, Gitali Roy |
| Length: | 139 minutes |

## 1966

*Nayak (The Hero)*

Producer: R.D.B. and Co.
Screenplay: Satyajit Ray
Photography: Subrata Mitra
Music: Satyajit Ray
Cast: Uttam Kumar, Sharmila Tagore, Bireswar Sen, Somen Bose, Nirmal Ghosh, Sumita Sanyal
Length: 120 minutes

## 1967

*Chiriakhana (The Zoo)*

Producer: Star Productions
Screenplay: Satyajit Ray (based on the novel *Chiriakhana* by Sharadindu Banerjee)
Photography: Soumendu Roy
Music: Satyajit Ray
Cast: Uttam Kumar, Sailen Mukherjee, Susil Majumdar, Kanika Majumdar, Shyamal Ghosal, Subhendu Chatterjee
Length: 125 minutes

## 1969

*Goopy Gyne Bagha Byne (The Adventures of Goopy and Bagha)*

Producer: Purnima Pictures
Screenplay: Satyajit Ray (based on a story by Upendrakishore Ray)
Photography: Soumendu Roy
Music: Satyajit Ray
Cast: Tapen Chatterjee, Rabi Ghosh, Santosh Dutta, Jahar Roy, Harindranath Chatterjee
Length: 132 minutes

## 1970

*Aranyer Din Ratri (Days and Nights in the Forest)*

Producer: Priya Films
Screenplay: Satyajit Ray (based on the novel *Aranyer Din Ratri* by Sunil Ganguly)

Photography: Soumendu Roy, Purnendu Bose
Music: Satyajit Ray
Cast: Soumitra Chatterjee, Subhendu Chatterjee, Samit Bhanja, Rabi Ghosh, Pahari Sanyal, Sharmila Tagore, Simi Garewal, Aparna Sen
Length: 115 minutes

## 1970

*Pratidwandi (The Adversary)*

Producer: Priya Films
Screenplay: Satyajit Ray (based on the novel *Pratidwandi* by Sunil Ganguly)
Photography: Soumendu Roy, Purnendu Bose
Music: Satyajit Ray
Cast: Dhritiman Chatterjee, Indira Devi, Debraj Roy, Krishna Bose, Jayashree Roy
Length: 110 minutes

## 1971

*Seemabaddha (Company Limited)*

Producer: Chitranjali
Screenplay: Satyajit Ray (based on the novel *Seemabaddha* by Shankar)
Photography: Soumendu Roy
Music: Satyajit Ray
Cast: Barun Chanda, Sharmila Tagore, Paromita Chowdhury, Haradhan Banerjee
Length: 112 minutes

## 1971

*Sikkim*

Producer: The Chogyal of Sikkim
Script and
Commentary: Satyajit Ray
Photography: Soumendu Roy
Music: Satyajit Ray
Length: 50 minutes

## 1972

*The Inner Eye*

    Producer: Films Division, Government of India
    Script and
    Commentary: Satyajit Ray
    Photography: Soumendu Roy
    Music: Satyajit Ray
    Length: 20 minutes

## 1973

*Ashani Sanket (Distant Thunder)*

    Producer: Balaka Movies
    Screenplay: Satyajit Ray (based on the novel *Ashani Sanket* by Bibhuti Bhusan Banerjee)
    Photography: Soumendu Roy
    Music: Satyajit Ray
    Cast: Soumitra Chatterjee, Babita, Sandhya Roy, Gobinda Chakravarti, Noni Ganguly
    Length: 101 minutes

## 1974

*Sonar Kella (The Golden Fortress)*

    Producer: Government of West Bengal
    Screenplay: Satyajit Ray (based on his novel *Sonar Kella*)
    Photography: Soumendu Roy
    Music: Satyajit Ray
    Cast: Soumitra Chatterjee, Santosh Dutta, Siddhartha Chatterjee, Kushal Chakravarti, Sailen Mukherjee, Ajoy Banerjee, Kamu Mukherjee
    Length: 120 minutes

## 1975

*Jana Aranya (The Middle Man)*

    Producer: Indus Films
    Screenplay: Satyajit Ray (based on the novel *Jana Aranya* by Shankar)
    Photography: Soumendu Roy

Music: Satyajit Ray
Cast: Pradip Mukherjee, Satya Banerjee, Dipankar Dey, Lily Chakravarti, Aparna Sen, Utpal Dutt, Rabi Ghosh
Length: 131 minutes

## 1976

*Bala*

Producer: National Center for the Performing Arts, Bombay, and Government of Tamil Nadu
Script and
Commentary: Satyajit Ray
Photography: Soumendu Roy
Music: Satyajit Ray
Length: 33 minutes

## 1977

*Shatranj ki Khilari (The Chess Players)*

Producer: Devki Chitra Productions
Screenplay: Satyajit Ray (based on the short story "Shatranj ki Khilari" by Prem Chand)
Photography: Soumendu Roy
Music: Satyajit Ray
Cast: Sanjeev Kumar, Saeed Jaffrey, Amjad Khan, Richard Attenborough, Shabana Azmi, Farida Jalal
Length: 113 minutes

## 1978

*Joi Baba Felunath (The Elephant God)*

Producer: R.D.B. and Co.
Screenplay: Satyajit Ray (based on his novel *Joi Baba Felunath*)
Photography: Soumendu Roy
Music: Satyajit Ray
Cast: Soumitra Chatterjee, Santosh Dutta, Siddhartha Chatterjee, Utpal Dutt, Jit Bose, Haradhan Banerjee, Biplab Chatterjee
Length: 112 minutes

## 1980

*Hirak Rajar Deshe (The Kingdom of Diamonds)*

      Producer: Government of West Bengal
  Screenplay: Satyajit Ray
Photography: Soumendu Roy
         Music: Satyajit Ray
          Cast: Soumitra Chatterjee, Utpal Dutta, Tapen Chatterjee, Rabi Ghosh
        Length: 118 minutes

## 1980

*Pikoo*

      Producer: Henri Fraise
  Screenplay: Satyajit Ray (based on his short story "Pikoor Diary")
Photography: Soumendu Roy
         Music: Satyajit Ray
          Cast: Arjun Guha Thakurta, Aparna Sen, Soven Lahiri, Promod Ganguli, Victor Banerjee
        Length: 26 minutes

## 1981

*Sadgati (Deliverance)*

      Producer: Doordarshan, Government of India
  Screenplay: Satyajit Ray (based on the short story "Sadgati" by Prem Chand)
Photography: Soumendu Roy
         Music: Satyajit Ray
          Cast: Om Puri, Smita Patil, Richa Mishra, Mohan Agashe
        Length: 26 minutes

## 1984

*Ghare Baire (The Home and the World)*

      Producer: National Film Developmen Corporation of India
  Screenplay: Satyajit Ray (based on the novel *Ghare Baire* by Rabindranath Tagore)

```
Photography: Soumendu Roy
     Music: Satyajit Ray
      Cast: Soumitra Chatterjee, Victor Banerjee, Swatilekha Chatter-
            jee, Gopa Aich, Jennifer Kapoor, Indrapramit Roy
    Length: 140 minutes
```

## 1987

*Sukumar Ray*

```
   Producer: Government of West Bengal
     Script: Satyajit Ray
 Commentary: Soumitra Chatterjee
Photography: Barun Raha
      Music: Satyajit Ray
       Cast: Soumitra Chatterjee, Utpal Dutt, Santosh Dutta, Tapen
             Chatterjee
     Length: 30 minutes
```

## 1989

*Ganashatru (An Enemy of the People)*

```
   Producer: National Film Development Corporation of India
 Screenplay: Satyajit Ray (based on the play An Enemy of the People by
             Henrik Ibsen)
Photography: Barun Raha
      Music: Satyajit Ray
       Cast: Soumitra Chatterjee, Ruma Guha Thakurta, Mamata
             Shankar, Dhritiman Chatterjee, Dipankar Dey, Subhendu
             Chatterjee
     Length: 100 minutes
```

## 1990

*Shakha Proshakha (Branches of a Tree)*

```
   Producer: Satyajit Ray Productions, Gerard Depardieu and Daniel
             Toscan Du Planter
 Screenplay: Satyajit Ray
Photography: Barun Raha
```

Music: Satyajit Ray
Cast: Promod Ganguli, Ajit Banerjee, Soumitra Chatterjee, Haradhan Banerjee, Dipankar Dey, Ranjit Mullick, Mamata Shankar
Length: 121 minutes

## 1991

*Agantuk (The Stranger)*

Producer: National Film Development Corporation of India
Screenplay: Satyajit Ray
Photography: Barun Raha
Music: Satyajit Ray
Cast: Utpal Dutt, Dipankar Dey, Mamata Shankar, Dhritiman Chatterjee
Length: 100 minutes

# Selected Bibliography

## Books

Armes, Roy. "Satyajit Ray," in *Third World Film Making and the West* (Berkeley: University of California Press, 1987), 231–42.

Cooper, Darius. "The Representation of Colonialism in Satyajit Ray's *The Chess Players*," in *Colonialism and Nationalism in Asian Cinema*, ed. Wimal Dissanayake (Bloomington: Indiana University Press, 1994), 174–89.

Das, Santi, ed. *Satyajit Ray: An Intimate Master* (Calcutta: Allied Publishers, 1998).

Das Gupta, Chidananda. *Satyajit Ray: An Anthology of Statements on Ray and by Ray* (New Delhi: Directorate of Film Festivals, 1981).

———. *The Cinema of Satyajit Ray* (New Delhi: Vikas, 1980; reprint, National Book Trust, 1994).

Datta, Alakananda, and Samik Bandyopadhyay, eds. *Satyajit Ray: A Film by Shyam Benegal* (Calcutta: Seagull Books, 1988).

Dissanayake, Wimal. "Art, Vision, and Culture: Satyajit Ray's Apu Trilogy Revisited," in *Cinema and Cultural Identity*, ed. Wimal Dissanayake (Lanham, MD: University Press of America, 1988), 93–106.

Kael, Pauline. "*Days and Nights in the Forest*," in *Reeling* (Boston: Little Brown, 1976), 140–43.

Kemp, Philip. "Satyajit Ray," in *World Film Directors*, Vol. II, ed. John Wakeman (New York: H.W. Wilson, 1988), 837–53.

Micciollo, Henri. *Satyajit Ray* (Lausanne: Editions L'Age d'Homme, 1981).

Nandy, Ashis. "An Intelligent Critic's Guide to Indian Cinema," in *Visual Anthropology and India*, ed. K.S. Singh (Calcutta: Anthropological Survey of India, 1992), 43–76.

Nyce, Ben. *Satyajit Ray: A Study of His Films* (New York: Praeger, 1988).

Rangoonwalla, Firoze. *Satyajit Ray's Art* (New Delhi: Clarion Books, 1980).

Ray, Satyajit. *Bishoy Chalachitra* (Calcutta: Ananda, 1976).

———. *The Apu Trilogy* (screenplays) (Calcutta: Seagull Books, 1985).

———. "My Life, My Work" in Tarapada Banerjee, *Satyajit Ray: A Portrait in Black and White* (New Delhi: Viking, 1993), 15–28.

———. *Our Films Their Films* (Hyderabad: Orient Longman, 1993).

———. *My Years with Apu* (New Delhi: Viking, 1994).

Roberge, Gaston. "Satyajit Ray: Humanism in the Cinema," in *Satyajit Ray Retrospective Souvenir: The Second Decade*, ed. Swapan Majumdar (Calcutta: n.p., 1979).

Robinson, Andrew. *Satyajit Ray: The Inner Eye* (Berkeley: University of California Press, 1989).

Russell Taylor, John. "Satyajit Ray," in *Cinema: A Critical Dictionary*, Vol. II, ed. Richard Roud (London: Secker and Warburg, 1980), 813–31.

Seton, Marie. *Satyajit Ray: Portrait of a Director* (London: Dennis Dobson, 1971).

Studlar, Gaylyn. "*Days and Nights in the Forest*," in *Magill's Survey of Cinema: Foreign Language Films*, Vol. II (Englewood Cliffs, NJ: Salem Hill Press, 1985), 746–51.

Tesson, Charles. *Satyajit Ray* (Paris: Cahiers du Cinema, 1992).

Wilson, David. "*Charulata*," in *Magill's Survey of Cinema: Foreign Language Films*, Vol. II (Englewood Cliffs, NJ: Salem Hill Press, 1985), 517–21.

Wood, Robin. *The Apu Trilogy* (New York: Praeger, 1971).

## Articles in Journals

Buruma, Ian. "The Last Bengali Renaissance Man." *New York Review of Books* 34, no. 18 (1987): 12–16.

Byron, Scott. "*Days and Nights in the Forest*." *Film Quarterly* 25, no.3 (1972): 36–37.

Cooper, Darius. "Colonialism in the Hindu Caste System: Satyajit Ray's *Sadgati*." *East–West Film Journal* 5, no. 2 (1991): 115–27.

———. "The Indian Woman in the Bengali/Hindu Dollhouse: Satyajit Ray's *Charulata*." *Women's Studies* 25 (1996): 189–200.

Das Gupta, Chidananda. "Ray and Tagore." *Sight and Sound* 36, no. 1 (1966–67): 30–34.

———. "*Charulata*." *Film Quarterly* 21, no. 1 (1967): 42–45.

Ganguly, Suranjan. "No Moksha: Arcadia Lost in Satyajit Ray's *Days and Nights in the Forest*." *Film Criticism* 19, no. 2 (1995): 75–85.

———. "Educating Ratan: The Politics of Masculinity in Satyajit Ray's *Postmaster*." *Toronto Review of Contemporary Writing Abroad* 13, no. 3 (1995): 70–77.

———. "In Search of India: Rewriting Self and Nation in Satyajit Ray's *Days and Nights in the Forest*." *Journal of South Asian Literature* 30, nos. 1–2 (1995): 162–72.

———. "Poetry into Prose: The Rewriting of Oudh in Satyajit Ray's *The Chess Players*." *Journal of Commonwealth Literature* 30, no. 2 (1995): 17–23.

Ghosh, Bishnupriya. "Satyajit Ray's *Devi*: Constructing a Third World Feminist Critique." *Screen* 33, no. 2 (1992): 165–73.

Hogan, Patrick. "Historical Economies of Race and Gender in Bengal: Ray and Tagore on *The Home and the World*." *Journal of South Asian Literature* 28, nos. 1–2 (1993): 23–44.

Houston, Penelope. "Ray's *Charulata*." *Sight and Sound* 35, no. 1 (1965–66): 31–33.

Kapur, Geeta. "Cultural Creativity in the First Decade: The Example of Satyajit Ray." *Journal of Arts and Ideas*, nos. 23–24 (1993): 17–49.

Kundu, Gautam. "Satyajit Ray, Rabindranath Tagore, and *The Home and the World*: Indian Nationalist History and the Colonial/Postcolonial Perspectives in Film and Fiction." *Asian Cinema* 9, no. 2 (1998): 53–68.

Malcolm, Derek. "Satyajit Ray." *Sight and Sound* 51, no. 2 (1982): 106–9.

Milne, Tom. "*Days and Nights in the Forest*." *Sight and Sound* 41, no. 1 (1971–72): 49.

———. "*The Adversary*." *Sight and Sound* 42, no. 2 (1973): 111.

Nandy, Ashis. "Satyajit Ray's Secret Guide to Exquisite Murders: Creativity, Social Criticism, and the Partitioning of the Self." *East–West Film Journal* 4, no. 2 (1990): 14–37.

———. "How 'Indian' Is Ray?" *Cinemaya* 20 (1993): 40–45.

Pritchett, Frances. "*The Chess Players*: From Premchand to Satyajit Ray." *Journal of South Asian Literature* 21, no. 2 (1986): 65–78.

Rajadhyaksha, Ashis. "Beyond Orientalism." *Sight and Sound* 2, no. 4 (1992): 32–35.

Ray, Bibekananda. "Ray Off Set." *Sight and Sound* 53, no. 1 (1983–84): 52–55.

Ray, Satyajit. "Under Western Eyes." *Sight and Sound* 51, no. 4 (1982): 268–74.

Rhode, Eric. "Satyajit Ray: A Study." *Sight and Sound* 30, no. 3 (1961): 132–36.

Ross, Alan. "Goodbye to Calcutta." *Telegraph Sunday Magazine* (Calcutta) (July 3, 1983): 10–11.

Schickel, Richard. "Days and Nights in the Art House." *Film Comment* 28, no. 3 (1992): 32–34.

Sen, Amartya. "Our Culture, Their Culture." *Telegraph* (Calcutta) (January 1 & 2, 1996): 8–9 and 10–11.

Singh, Madan Gopal. "Ray and the Realist Conscience." *Cinemaya* 20 (1993): 46–48.

Singh, Nikky-Guninder Kaur. "From Flesh to Stone: The Divine Metamorphosis in Satyajit Ray's *Devi*." *Journal of South Asian Literature* 28, nos. 1–2 (1993): 227–50.

Wong, Fran. "Ray's *Mahanagar*: Arati Chooses Integrity Over Security." *Cineaction* 30 (1993): 24–35.

## Interviews

Allen, Wendy, and Roger Spikes. "Satyajit Ray." *Stills* 1 (1981): 40–48.

Andersson, Kerstin. "Satyajit Ray." *Cinema Papers* 88 (1992): 44–50.

Blue, James. "Satyajit Ray." *Film Comment* 4, no. 4 (1968): 4–15.

Ganguly, Suranjan. "One Single Blend: A Conversation with Satyajit Ray." *East–West Film Journal* 3, no. 2 (1989): 91–95.

Gray, Hugh. "Satyajit Ray." *Film Quarterly* 12, no. 2 (1958): 4–7.

Gupta, Udayan. "The Politics of Humanism." *Cineaste* 12, no. 1 (1982): 24–29.

Hughes, John. "A Voyage in India." *Film Comment* 12, no. 5 (1976): 52–54.

Issakson, Folke. "Conversation with Satyajit Ray." *Sight and Sound* 39, no. 3 (1970): 114–20.

Neveu, Jean. "Ray on Renoir." *Amis Indiens* (Bombay) 3 (1978–79): 33–36.

Ray, Satyajit. "Dialogue on Film." *American Film* 3, no. 9 (1978): 39–50.

Roy, Karuna Shankar. "The Artist in Politics: From an Interview with Satyajit Ray in *Kolkata*, May 1970." *Drama Review* 15, no. 2 (1971): 310.

Thomsen, Christian Braad. "Ray's New Trilogy." *Sight and Sound* 42, no. 1 (1972–73): 31–33.

# Index

# About the Author

**SURANJAN GANGULY** is from Calcutta, India, and studied at St. Xavier's College and Jadavpur University before coming to the United States. He received his doctorate degree from Purdue University, Indiana, and currently teaches European and Asian cinema at the University of Colorado at Boulder. He was chair of Film Studies from 2000 to 2005. His work has appeared in *Sight and Sound, Film Criticism, East-West Film Journal, The Journal of Commonwealth Literature, Michigan Quarterly Review, Ariel, The Toronto Review of Contemporary Writing Abroad, Journal of South Asian Literature,* and *Asian Cinema.* He is completing a study of the films of Adoor Gopalakrishnan, one of India's most distinguished contemporary filmmakers. He can be reached by e-mail at ganguly@stripe.colorado.edu.